Soft Rebel, Untamed Life

Choosing Self Over Hustle Culture

By Fickle Flashes Collective

Copyright © 2025 by Fickle Flashes LLC
All rights reserved.

Published under the creative studio **Fickle Flashes Collective.**

Some names, details, and identifying characteristics have been changed to protect the privacy of individuals. Certain scenes and stories are composite or inspired by real experiences but have been adapted for narrative clarity.

No part of this book may be reproduced, stored in a retrieval system, or transmitted in any form or by any means—electronic, mechanical, photocopying, recording, or otherwise—without the express written permission of the publisher, except for brief quotations used in reviews or articles.

Cover design by Fickle Flashes Collective | AI Assisted

Published by Fickle Flashes Press
An imprint of Fickle Flashes LLC

San Diego, California

ISBN: 979-8-9999161-5-0

Printed in the United States of America

Dedication

To those who refuse the noise, who carve space for breath,
who know that wildness and rest can live side by side—
this is for you.

Contents

Introduction: Welcome to the Soft Rebellion 1
Chapter 1: The Myth of More 11
Chapter 2: The High Price of 'On' 21
Chapter 3: The Social Performance Trap............................ 29
Chapter 4: Redefining Success... 37
Chapter 5: The Art of Doing Nothing 47
Chapter 6: Cultivating Authenticity 59
Chapter 7: Living Out Loud, Soft Rebel Style 69
Chapter 8: Embracing Imperfection 77
Chapter 9: Your Career, Your Way 85
Chapter 10: The Financial Rebellion.................................. 94
Chapter 11: Building Your Village: The Rebellion of Connection 105
Chapter 12: Reclaiming the Body...................................... 119
Chapter 13: Creating Your Sanctuary 129
Chapter 14: Your Personal Manifesto 141
Chapter 15: The Quiet Revolution Continues 149
Chapter 16: A New Beginning 155
Epilogue: Still Becoming 163
    Notes and Sources: 168

Introduction: Welcome to the Soft Rebellion

✦ ✦ ✦

An invitation to slow down, untangle the noise, and remember that softness is not surrender.

Welcome to the Untamed Life

This book is an invitation to live more intentionally, to move through the world with authenticity instead of autopilot, and to release the weight of expectations that were never yours to carry. It's not about shrinking down or staying quiet—it's about showing up in a way that feels true, even when that looks different from what the world demands.

Before we go any further, I want to be honest with you: I am still very much a work in progress. I didn't write this book from some perfect place on the other side of struggle. I wrote it while in the middle of it—while learning, unlearning, stumbling, and trying again. The practices and insights here are rooted in research and lived experience, but I still wrestle with them daily. Like you, I'm figuring it out as I go.

That's part of what it means to be a soft rebel: to choose authenticity in the middle of the mess, not after everything has been perfected. I'm not offering polished answers or quick fixes. What I'm offering is what has helped me, in the hope that some of it may help you too.

Together, we can push back against the cultural scripts that tell us we must always do more, be more, prove more. Instead, we can choose slower, truer, more deliberate ways of being—and trust that this, too, is powerful.

So, stop. Take a deep breath.

If you're reading this, you've likely felt it—that low hum of anxiety that follows you from your desk to your dinner table, the nagging feeling that you should always be doing more, the exhaustion of a life spent chasing an ever-moving finish line. We've all been sold a story of success built on a relentless foundation: work harder, scale faster, grind longer. We call it "the hustle." And for a long time, we all bought in. We pushed ourselves to the brink, convinced that more productivity, more money, and more "likes" would finally lead to fulfillment.

But no matter your age, the promised land of success has turned out to be a desert of burnout and emptiness.

Why Hustle Feels So Heavy

Burnout isn't just a buzzword—it's a physiological state. The **World Health Organization** recognizes it as an occupational phenomenon marked by exhaustion, mental distance from one's work, and reduced professional efficacy. When we are constantly "on," our nervous system lives in a state of **sympathetic activation**—the fight-or-flight mode designed for short bursts of survival. When stress lingers, hormones such as cortisol and adrenaline stay elevated. Over time, this constant surge strains the body—blood pressure climbs, digestion goes off balance, and restful sleep becomes harder to find (NET Australia, 2022)

This isn't sustainable, yet it has become our default. Studies show that chronic stress increases the risk of anxiety, depression, cardiovascular disease, and weakened immunity. What we casually call "hustle culture" is, at its core, a system that keeps our biology in a state of perpetual alarm.

💭 **Science Note:** The human body was designed for cycles of exertion and rest. Without recovery, the nervous system never resets—leading to chronic exhaustion and burnout (McEwen, 1998; Sonnentag & Fritz, 2015; Maslach & Leiter, 1997).

A Different Kind of Power

This book is not another guide on how to be a better worker. It's not about optimizing your schedule or building a six-figure side hustle. Instead, it's about a different kind of power—the power of **Soft Rebellion**.

Soft Rebellion is the quiet act of choosing to live your life on your own terms. It's a gentle but firm refusal to accept a one-size-fits-all definition of success. It's the art of finding your own pace and your own purpose, even when the world around you is sprinting.

The Generational Lens

Your journey to this point is unique, shaped by the decade you came of age:

- **Baby Boomers** were taught that loyalty and hard work were the keys to a stable life. You showed up early, stayed late, and poured yourself into careers. But many now feel the disillusionment of realizing decades of sacrifice didn't guarantee peace. This book is for you—to help you build a legacy of joy and authenticity rather than endless effort.

- **Generation X** came of age with skepticism, questioning authority and distrusting the corporate ladder. But mortgages, families, and careers buried that rebellious heart. This book is a way to reclaim it—helping you navigate the system without losing yourself.

- **Millennials** inherited instability and adopted a culture of hustle, embracing side gigs and online performance. You are the ultimate optimizers—and the most burned out. This book is your permission slip to step off the hamster wheel and seek a life that feels full, rather than just busy.

- **Generation Z** spotted the flaws early. You value authenticity and mental health, but bills and responsibilities still require strategy. This book shows you how to channel your rebellious spirit into a peaceful, sustainable way of living.

Each generation wrestles with the same cultural pressure, filtered through its own lens. No matter your age, this book is here to help you reclaim a different rhythm.

Why We're Exhausted

In a world that tells us to hustle, to be always on, and to constantly seek more, many of us find ourselves in a state of **perpetual exhaustion**. We carry the weight of demanding careers, the pressure of a perfectly curated social media presence, and the unspoken anxiety of never being good enough.

Researchers often describe this as the "hedonic treadmill"—our tendency to quickly adapt to new achievements and immediately crave the next. (Diener, Lucas, & Scollon, 2006). No matter how much we do, the satisfaction fades, and the cycle begins again. Pair this with the dopamine-driven pull of technology, and it's no wonder so many feel depleted, isolated, and disconnected from their own lives.

The root of this problem is the hustle itself. We have been conditioned to believe that our worth is measured by our productivity, our success by our busyness, and our value by our endless output. We are told to grind, to optimize, and to climb a ladder that often leads to a life we don't even want.

In this relentless pursuit, we lose ourselves. We lose our peace, our purpose, and our ability to simply be present.

☑ **Permission Slip:** Your worth is not your output.

A Gentle Revolution

But there is another way.

This book is a guide to unwind, a gentle yet powerful rebellion against the toxic culture of "more." It is not a call to quit your job or abandon your ambitions. Instead, it is an invitation to redefine them on your own terms.

Soft Rebel, Untamed Life is a quiet revolution of intentionality—the choice to live a life of purpose over performance, peace over possessions, and presence over productivity.

Over the coming chapters, we will explore how to:

- Redefine success to align with your personal values, not the world's expectations.
- Reclaim rest as a non-negotiable part of your life, without guilt.
- Achieve financial peace and break free from the cycle of constant consumption.
- Build a supportive community that fuels you, rather than a network that drains you.
- Create physical and mental sanctuaries that protect you from the noise of the world.

This journey is a return to a more natural, human rhythm. It is a path to reclaim your time, your energy, and ultimately, your life.

The world is waiting for you to begin your soft rebellion.

The world is loud, but your rebellion doesn't have to look one way. It can be a whisper, a laugh, a bold choice, or a quiet exhale. It can be messy, vibrant, or serene. What matters is that it is yours.

Your rebellion starts now.

✨ A Few Notes from Your Fellow Soft Rebel

You might have already noticed a few recurring signposts tucked through these pages — a *Permission Slip* here, a *Cozy Victory* there. They're small pauses along the way — part reflection, part reset — to help you take what you need and leave the rest.

Here's what each one means, in case you like knowing the map before the journey.

💭 Science Note
A quick, compassionate dive into what's happening beneath the surface — the psychology, neuroscience, or behavioral patterns behind our very human tendencies. These aren't lectures; they're little "ohhh, that makes sense" moments to help you understand your mind with more kindness.

● Cozy Victory
Tiny wins that deserve a standing ovation. A Cozy Victory celebrates the small, often invisible triumphs — washing the dishes *and* walking away before burnout, setting a boundary, or simply choosing not to multitask. Rebellion can be quiet and still count.

☑ Permission Slip
Your official pass to be human. These slips give you permission to pause, rest, or say no — to remember that slowing down isn't failure, it's strategy.

✿ Soft Rebel Move
A gentle experiment in living differently. Each Soft Rebel Move offers a practical way to apply what you've read — something small but meaningful to shift how you show up, plan, or rest. It's rebellion in motion, minus the pressure to perfect it.

Rebel Reflection

Open-ended questions meant to stir, not solve. They're invitations to notice what's shifting, what's true, and what you might be ready to release.

Take what resonates. Skip what doesn't. This isn't homework — it's a shared field guide for untaming your life, one soft act at a time.

Chapter 1: The Myth of More

✦ ✦ ✦

 A soft rebellion begins where the wanting quiets.

In Chapter 1, we will examine the engine driving this exhaustion: the myth that more is always better.

Now that we understand the toll of the "always on" life, let us examine the cultural story that got us here.

The first step in any rebellion is to understand what you're fighting. In our case, that's not a person or an institution, but an idea—a story so deeply woven into our lives that we mistake it for fact. I call it **The Myth of More.**

This myth is a simple, powerful blueprint for a life where success is measured by a single metric: relentless, constant forward motion. It tells us that more is always better. More productivity, more income, more possessions, more accolades. We have all become students of this myth, driven by a fear that if we're not constantly doing, we're falling behind.

My Costa Rica Wake-Up Call

I learned this lesson the hard way years ago in Costa Rica.

We were staying near a national park, and the whole point of the trip was to slow down—poolside naps, easy beach days, the kind of relaxation you swear you need but never give yourself. At the time, my career was really starting to take off. I'd been promoted, and I was laser-focused on climbing the ladder.

So, of course, when we arrived, we couldn't just "do nothing." The first few days were a blur of hiking trails, walking into town, shopping, checking out every restaurant we could find, and signing up for every activity offered. One day, we booked a zipline tour—soaring through the trees, rappelling down platforms, racing to squeeze in one more thrill.

And then it happened. On one of the last rappels, the rope ripped across my lower back and left me with the worst rope burn imaginable. I couldn't hike. I couldn't swim. I couldn't even sit comfortably in a beach chair. For the rest of the trip, I was basically grounded.

At first, I was furious. My body had betrayed me, slowing me down when I had so much "fun" scheduled. But then something shifted. We stumbled into a little shop that loaned out books. I picked one up, and that was it: my days turned into hours of reading, resting, and simply being still as my back healed.

It was uncomfortable at first—not just the injury, but the silence. No TV. No itinerary. No endless checklist of things to conquer. But somewhere between the ointment, the pages, and the naps, I felt something I hadn't in a long time: peace.

- **Cozy Victory:** Being forced to stay in with a book turned out to be the best part of the trip.

- **Soft Rebel Move:** Let life slow you down before burnout does.

Why "More" Never Feels Like Enough

In the past, the pressure to "keep up with the Joneses" was a local battle fought over a manicured lawn or a new car. Today, thanks to the constant scroll of our phones, we are caught in a global competition with literal strangers. We are bombarded with a curated highlight reel of other people's perfect vacations, seamless careers, and flawless families. This creates a new and insidious form of anxiety—the gnawing fear that no matter how much we achieve, it will never be enough. Our sense of self-worth becomes tied to a performance that we can never win, trapping us in a cycle of comparison and chronic self-doubt.

Spoiler: More isn't more. It's just more.

🧠 **Science Note:** Psychologists call this **social comparison theory**—our natural drive to measure ourselves against others (Festinger, 1954). In the age of social media, comparison is constant, which research links to higher rates of anxiety, depression, and dissatisfaction (Appel et al., 2016; Twenge et al., 2018).

You know this feeling. Sunday night rolls around, and your list still has a dozen things unchecked. You tell yourself the whole weekend was a wash. Or that pang of guilt when you sink into the couch for ten quiet minutes, doing absolutely nothing. Somewhere along the way, we stopped treating busyness as just busyness. Now it's become bragging rights. A jammed calendar isn't proof of a rich life—it's just proof that you never stop moving.

☑️ **Permission Slip:** You don't have to answer emails at 10 p.m.. The world will keep spinning.

The Culture of Performative Hustle

This myth has created the culture of performative hustle. In our professional lives, it's not just about doing the work, but being seen doing the work—answering emails at odd hours, taking on more projects than you can handle, and even competing for the title of "first one in, last one out." In our personal lives, this same energy is applied to our hobbies, our health, and even our vacations. Leisure has to be productive; a relaxing trip isn't enough unless it's an "adventure" for our social media feeds. Your value is no longer inherent; it's determined by your output.

And what happens when we tie our sense of worth to our output? We break.

Alex's Story

I knew a man named Alex, a high-pressure PM with a thriving side hustle, who was the living embodiment of the myth of more. He also had a perfectly curated social life that looked incredible. His highlight reels made you jealous. On a rare day off, he wouldn't just relax; he'd have to hike a mountain, then try to read a 500-page book in one sitting, all while planning his next big move. He once told me, with a strange mix of pride and exhaustion, "I don't know how to just be."

The myth of more just kept running him ragged, like an engine that never shut off. But it couldn't last—it never does. Suddenly, his calendar was wide open, but instead of relief, he felt a pit of anxiety. On paper, he had everything people said would make him successful. In reality, he was worn down and miserable. The "more" he chased never filled the gap. If anything, it left him chasing harder, thinking maybe the next thing would finally be enough. The problem with a life spent chasing more is that you're never present for the life you already have.

Honestly, exhaustion isn't a trophy—it's a warning light.

The First Act of Soft Rebellion

The first act of soft rebellion, then, is to simply see this myth for what it is. It's not a secret formula for success; it's a trap. It's a story that tells us to ignore the quiet wisdom of our own bodies and minds in favor of external validation. It's a cruel game designed to keep us running just fast enough to avoid asking the questions that really matter: What is enough? What brings me joy? What does a life of purpose, on my own terms, actually look like?

☑ **Permission Slip:** You're allowed to leave a task unfinished and still be worthy.

Performing Our Lives

This myth of "more" isn't abstract—it's alive in the small moments, whispering in the background of how we live. It's the voice that tells you your weekend was wasted because you didn't learn a new skill or do something that is considered "productive". It's the anxiety that whispers you're falling behind every time you see a friend's shiny new life update on social media. We've all been trained to believe that the opposite of "more" is "less," and that "less" is a one-way ticket to failure. We see a life of stillness not as peace, but as a sign of apathy.

Think about it. We have become experts at optimizing our lives. We have apps to track our sleep, water intake, steps, finances, and focus time. We follow morning routines designed by billionaires and try to replicate them in our tiny apartments, all before our first cup of coffee. We believe that if we just get the right system, the right app, or the right mindset, we will finally crack the code to an effortless, perfect life.

We don't need another tracker. We need a break.

But what if the code is a lie?

🧠 **Science Note:** This is sometimes called the **Productivity Paradox**—the phenomenon where efficiency tools (apps, email, AI) actually increase workload instead of reducing it. Time saved is rarely spent resting; it's consumed by new demands (Brynjolfsson, 1993; Mazmanian et al., 2013).

The myth of more is particularly insidious because it exploits our innate desire for security and happiness. The more we do, the more we have to do. The more we earn, the more we are expected to earn. Our calendars become a badge of honor, a public declaration of how important and in-demand we are. We become addicted to the rush of being "busy," even when we know in our hearts that the busyness is a distraction from what truly matters. We are performing our lives, not living them.

✊ **Soft Rebel Move:** Cancel one meeting this week. Notice how the world doesn't end.

This "performance" seeps into every corner of our existence. Our personal lives become another stage for the myth of more. A relaxing weekend isn't enough; it must be an "adventure" for our social media feeds. A quiet evening at home feels unproductive unless we're multitasking—watching a movie while answering emails. Even our hobbies are no longer about enjoyment; they're about becoming the "best" at something or turning our passion into a side business. A simple walk isn't a walk; it's a step-tracking exercise. A vacation isn't rest, it's a curated photo shoot. We've been conditioned to believe that our leisure must also be productive, a quantifiable achievement that proves our worth.

☑ **Permission Slip:** A walk can just be a walk.

The Hunger Beneath "More"

The problem isn't our desire for a better life; it's the definition of "better." The myth of more teaches us to chase external rewards—the bigger house, the fancier car, the impressive job title. But these things are like water through a sieve. They don't fill the void. They can't, because the void isn't a physical space that can be filled with stuff. It's a hunger for something more profound: for meaning, for connection, and for peace.

The first act of soft rebellion is to simply acknowledge this. It's to look at the relentless pursuit of more and say, "I see you, but I'm not playing that game anymore." It's about recognizing that constant activity doesn't equal progress, and a full calendar doesn't equal a full life. This is not about becoming lazy or giving up on ambition. Instead, it's about a radical act of re-evaluation. It's the moment you choose to put down the weight of external expectations and ask yourself a simple, terrifying question: *"What is enough?"*

A Browser with a Hundred Tabs

Perhaps you've already felt the quiet pull of this rebellion. I recently had a friend who, by all accounts, was a model student of the myth of more. She had a high-powered job, an impressive social life, and a perfectly apartment. She was always on, always connected, always moving forward. The company she kept and the life she led were a testament to her success. But every now and then, I'd see a flash of something else—a moment of profound exhaustion in her eyes. The myth of more was demanding a price, and it was a price she wasn't sure she could keep paying.

One evening, after a particularly demanding week, she didn't show up for our usual Friday night gathering. We were all worried, but she simply texted, "I'm staying in. I'm just... sitting." The next day, she explained it. "My brain felt like a browser with a hundred open tabs," she said. "I just needed to close them all."

This was her first act of soft rebellion. It wasn't loud or dramatic; it was just a quiet decision to opt out.

- **Cozy Victory:** Choosing to sit instead of perform is sometimes the bravest act of all.

Rebel Reflection: Spotting the Myth of More

- Where in your daily life do you feel pressured to chase "more"?
- When was the last time you did something just because it brought you joy—not because it looked impressive?

- What would change if you believed "enough" was truly enough?

Chapter 2: The High Price of 'On'

✦ ✦ ✦

We were never meant to live at full brightness.
Even stars know when to dim.

In our last chapter, we examined the myth of more, a powerful blueprint for a life of relentless forward motion. It's a compelling story, but it leaves out a crucial part: the receipt. The myth promises an effortless climb to the top, but it hides the cost of the ticket. And that cost is your emotional, physical, and mental well-being.

The price of being "on" is often paid in silence, a quiet suffering that our culture doesn't have a place for. We've been trained to power through, to push past the "little" signals our bodies and minds are sending. A tight chest. A racing mind that won't shut off. A complete lack of interest in the things that used to bring us joy. These aren't just minor inconveniences; they are the warning lights on the dashboard of your life. And ignoring them is a direct path to a full-blown breakdown.

Permission Slip: You're allowed to pull over when the warning lights flash.

The most common consequence of the myth of more is burnout. Burnout isn't just being tired—it's the point where stress grinds you down so completely that your body, your mind, and your emotions all wave the white flag. Picture a car that's been pushed in the red for too long—eventually, the engine gives out. That's what burnout feels like. It's more than fatigue; it's cynicism creeping in, a dull sense of detachment from the work that once mattered, and the hollow feeling that no achievement is ever enough. At its core, burnout is what happens when we've been taught to value output more than our own well-being.

Burnout (that WHO-defined state of exhaustion and mental distance we covered in the Introduction) is not weakness—it is biology reacting to overload.

Soft Rebel Move: Step away before the engine seizes. Rest is maintenance, not indulgence.

And then there's anxiety, the constant hum that accompanies the hustle. For many, it's not a sudden panic attack, but a low-level, continuous state of fight-or-flight. This is the body's ancient alarm system screaming that something is wrong, even when on the surface, everything looks fine. Being in this state leads to a host of physical problems, from sleepless nights and a compromised immune system to a perpetual knot in your stomach.

living in fight-or-flight isn't a personality trait.

Science Note: The **sympathetic nervous system** (fight-or-flight) was designed for short bursts of survival. When activated constantly, it disrupts sleep cycles, raises cortisol, and prevents the body from entering repair mode (McEwen, 2007).

Beyond these well-known conditions, the hustle takes a direct, physical toll on our bodies. The stress hormones, cortisol and adrenaline, which are designed to save us in a moment of crisis, become a constant presence. Our bodies are not meant to run on this fuel forever. This chronic state of high alertness can lead to inflammation, digestive issues, and a constant state of muscle tension. Imagine wearing a suit of armor that never comes off. We feel these symptoms but dismiss them as just part of being an adult. We pop a pill for the headache, drink another coffee for the fatigue, and tell ourselves, "This is just how it is." We've normalized a constant state of physical and emotional dis-ease.

- **Cozy Victory:** Taking the armor off for even one evening—hot shower, pajamas, no agenda—is a win.

Perhaps the most insidious part of the myth is the concept of moral productivity. Our value as human beings has become tied to our output. We are judged by our colleagues, our families, and our social media feeds on how busy we are, how much we've accomplished, and how "full" our lives appear. As a result, we've come to believe that being productive is inherently "good" and that resting is not just unproductive, but a moral failing. The very act of doing nothing can create a powerful wave of guilt and anxiety. We've become so afraid of being perceived as lazy or apathetic that we avoid stillness at all costs, even when our bodies are begging for it.

- **Science Note:** This is what psychologists term moral productivity bias—the belief that "busy equals good." Studies show this bias increases guilt when people rest, even when rest improves performance and health (Hafenbrack & Mogilner, 2021).

- **Permission Slip:** Rest is not laziness. Doing nothing is doing something.

I learned the price of "on" the hard way. For a year, my life was a relentless cycle of travel and projects. I got up early to make my flight, and flew home late in the day. I was exhausted, but in my new role, I wanted to show my value.

Then, one evening, after weeks of nonstop travel, I was driving home from the airport. I was physically drained, and this was my regular schedule. Suddenly, my heart began to race. My arms felt tingly and then went numb. My fingers cramped up, and I couldn't seem to draw a full breath. I truly believed I was dying. In a sheer act of will, I managed to pull the car over. My hands were so locked up that I couldn't use them to dial my phone; I had to use my knuckles to punch in 911.

The paramedics arrived, and after checking me over, they gave me the diagnosis: a panic attack.

Soft Rebel Move: Listen when your body whispers, so it doesn't have to scream.

That moment was not a sign of failure; it was an act of mercy. My body was staging its own rebellion, a definitive and terrifying "no" after years of quiet pleas. It was the moment my physical being refused to carry the psychological weight of the hustle any longer. It was the final, unavoidable symptom of a life lived for the myth of more.

The Mental Health Toll of "Always On"

My panic attack wasn't an isolated event—it was my body's way of staging a rebellion. And I'm not alone. Across the world, mental health challenges have been rising steadily, with many researchers pointing to our "always on" culture as a major driver.

- The **World Health Organization** reports that rates of anxiety and depression increased by **25% globally during the first year of the pandemic**, but the trend started long before COVID (World Health Organization, 2022).

- In the U.S., the **American Psychological Association** consistently finds that chronic workplace stress and "constant availability" are top contributors to burnout and mental health strain.

- Young adults—especially Millennials and Gen Z—report the highest levels of stress, with many saying they feel pressure to be productive even in their free time.

Being "always on" blurs the line between work and life until there is no line at all. The notifications never stop, the performance never pauses, and our nervous systems never get a chance to reset. Over time, this constant stimulation erodes not only our energy but also our ability to feel joy, calm, and focus.

🧠 **Science Note:** Research confirms that chronic stress physically changes the brain, shrinking the hippocampus (which affects memory) and over-activating the amygdala (which heightens fear and anxiety) (McEwen, 2007; Lupien et al., 2009).

This chapter is not meant to scare you, but to give a name to what you may have been feeling all along. This is to validate the anxiety you've been carrying, the exhaustion you've been ignoring, and the emptiness you may have felt. These are not signs of weakness; they are evidence that you are a human being, not a machine. They are the first whispers of your soft rebellion. By simply acknowledging the cost, you've taken the first step toward healing and toward finding a path that is not just more, but better.

Rebel Reflection: The Cost of "On"

- When do you feel the "warning lights" in your body?
- What would it look like to take them seriously instead of pushing through?
- Where have you tied your worth to productivity—and how could you begin to untangle that?

Chapter 3: The Social Performance Trap

✦ ✦ ✦

Somewhere between who we are and who we show, we start performing what we once felt.

If the myth of more is the engine of our discontent, then the social performance trap is the fuel. We've already seen how the hustle can lead to burnout and anxiety, but where does a lot of that pressure come from? It comes from the outside, from the relentless, unavoidable, and often edited lives we see playing out all around us. In a world where everyone is a performer, we can easily lose ourselves in the audience.

The pressure to be perfect is not new, but technology has turned it into a full-time job. With a single tap, we can filter our flaws, crop out our mess, and meticulously curate a highlight reel of a life we may not actually be living. We are told to brand ourselves, to build a public persona, and to present a flawless version of ourselves for the world to consume. This continuous performance is not only exhausting but also a profound source of anxiety. It creates a constant fear of being "found out," of having our messy, imperfect reality exposed to a judgmental audience. The need to be authentic is more critical than ever, because the cost of faking it has never been higher.

☑ **Permission Slip:** You don't have to filter your life into something it's not.

The way we experience this pressure is deeply tied to the generation we grew up in.

For Baby Boomers and Generation X, this performance trap began on a local scale. It was the classic "keeping up with the Joneses." You might remember your parents or grandparents talking about it—Bob and Carol next door got a new car, or your friend from work just put in a pool. The competition was real, but it was also contained. You could go inside, close the blinds, and for a little while, you were disconnected from the pressure. The world didn't follow you home. For these generations, the technology that amplified this trap came on quickly, a firehose of information in a world that wasn't prepared for it.

But for Millennials and Generation Z, the story is entirely different. For many, a digital connection has been a part of life from the very beginning. The pressure to perform isn't just from the people next door; it's from every corner of the planet, accessible in your pocket 24/7. Your friend's vacation in Bali is just a tap away, as is an influencer's perfect new home, or a college acquaintance's impressive career promotion. The stage is no longer your neighborhood; it's the entire globe, and the performance never ends.

the Joneses aren't next door anymore—they're in Bali, and they have a ring light.

🗨 **Science Note:** According to Pew Research, **95% of U.S. teens have access to a smartphone**, and nearly half say they are online "almost constantly." The **average adult spends over 2.5 hours per day on social media**, while teens often spend double that amount. Heavy use is consistently linked with higher rates of anxiety, depression, and sleep disruption (Pew Research Center, 2022; DataReportal, 2023; Twenge & Campbell, 2018).

My therapist once shared an analogy that perfectly captures this reality: we are like sponges. We can only absorb so much information until we start to leak. The constant flood of curated images, success stories, and highlight reels from social media is far more than a mind can hold. It seeps into our subconscious, leaking out as anxiety, self-doubt, and a constant, low-grade feeling of inadequacy. We are saturated with the performances of others, but starved of our own authentic experience.

- **Cozy Victory:** Closing the app and opening a book instead.

The biggest lie of the social performance trap is the myth of the "curated online self." What we see is not a life; it's a series of carefully selected moments designed to create a specific perception. Influencers aren't just selling products; they're selling a fantasy of a perfect life, and we buy into it, believing that our messy, unedited reality is somehow a failure. We see a friend's perfect family photo and forget the tantrum that happened five minutes before it was taken. We see the promotion, but we don't see the long nights, the stress, and the moments of profound self-doubt that led to it.

This is the significant gap between our curated online selves and our messy, authentic reality. And it's in this gap that our anxiety thrives. We are left comparing our behind-the-scenes to everyone else's highlight reel. The old "keeping up with the Joneses" was a competition you could at least take a break from. Today, the Joneses have a million followers, are on vacation in a different country every month, and are always ready with a perfectly posed, professionally edited update.

- **Soft Rebel Move:** Compare less, connect more.

The emotional toll of this comparison is profound. It's not just a momentary pang of jealousy; it's a constant, subconscious scorecard on which we are always losing. We measure our accomplishments, our relationships, and our bodies against an impossible, doctored ideal, and the result is a relentless current of self-doubt. This leads to a profound sense of FOMO—the fear of missing out—which is really a fear of being left behind, of being irrelevant. As we introduced in Chapter 1's science note on social comparison, the feed keeps score for us—here's how it morphs into FOMO in practice. We feel compelled to participate, to post, and to perform, not because we want to, but because we are terrified of what might happen if we don't. The very technology that was supposed to connect us has become a tool of our own isolation and judgment.

Spoiler: FOMO is just the fear of being human.

🌐 **Science Note:** Studies show that **FOMO is highest among young adults**, but rising in every generation. In one survey, **56% of social media users** admitted feeling afraid they would miss something if they didn't check their feeds. This constant checking keeps the brain in a dopamine-driven loop of seeking validation (Przybylski et al., 2013; Eventbrite & Harris Poll, 2014; Meshi et al., 2015).

The Email Spiral

It doesn't just happen on Instagram. I've lived the performance trap in my work, too. Back before Grammarly and AI tools, writing the "perfect" email was its own full-time job. I couldn't even count the hours I spent drafting and redrafting messages, especially those where I had to disagree with someone or deliver news I knew they wouldn't want to hear.

Those emails became projects in themselves. I'd write a version, then rewrite it, then ask a colleague to "take a look" before sending. By the time it finally went out, the energy I had spent crafting it could've fueled an entire presentation.

And here's the thing: most of the time, the other person barely responded. A quick "thanks" or "got it" was all I'd get back. Meanwhile, I'd invested half a day in trying to perfect something that didn't need to be perfect at all.

Soft Rebel Move: Stop editing the email for the eleventh time. Hit send.

This social performance trap is a vicious cycle. It often begins with a trigger—seeing a friend's perfectly framed vacation photo. Your brain, wired for social comparison, immediately performs a cost-benefit analysis of your own life, and the result is a feeling of inadequacy. The emotional response is self-doubt, a gnawing question of "Why not me?" Then, the cycle prompts an action: you work harder, you book a similar trip, or you stage your own "perfect" moment to post, hoping to get the same validation. When the likes and comments come in, you get a small dopamine hit, but the relief is fleeting. Because within minutes, you'll see someone else's highlight reel, and the whole cycle begins again. It's a feedback loop of anxiety that serves no one but the platforms that profit from our constant engagement.

🍵 **Science Note:** Neuroscience research shows that each "like" or notification releases a small burst of **dopamine**, the brain's reward chemical. However, the effect is short-lived, keeping us hooked in a cycle of checking, scrolling, and posting in search of the next hit (Meshi, Tamir, & Heekeren, 2015; Montag & Heinz, 2018).

✅ **Permission Slip:** You don't have to perform your life for an audience. Living it is enough.

The first step in escaping this trap is to recognize it for what it is—a performance. It's to understand that what you're seeing is not a life, but a piece of content. The true rebellion begins not with a bold post, but with a quiet decision: to stop performing, to put down the phone, and to be present in your own real, unfiltered life, in all its imperfect beauty. This is a difficult first step because it requires you to be okay with not being seen, to be content with your own truth, even if it doesn't get a single like or comment. It's a refusal to play a game you cannot win.

● **Cozy Victory:** Choosing to sit in your messy living room, phone face down, and actually enjoy your evening.

🕊 Rebel Reflection: Escaping the Social Performance Trap

- Where do you find yourself curating instead of just living?
- What triggers your comparison spiral most often?

- How would it feel to share less—or not share at all—and still feel whole?
- What's one area of your life you'd like to reclaim from performance into authenticity?
- If no one could see your resume, bank balance, or social media feed, how would you define success?
- How might rewriting your scorecard shift what you model for your children, your team, or your friends?

Closing

Redefining success is not just about living differently—it's about breaking a cycle. The scorecards we follow today will shape the scorecards the next generation inherits. By choosing peace over hustle, connection over comparison, and presence over performance, we don't just rewrite our lives; we transform them. We rewrite what "success" looks like for those who come after us.

Your quiet rebellion starts here: draft your scorecard, live by it, and revise it as often as you need. Success isn't a destination. It's a practice.

And the most successful life is the one that feels like yours.

Chapter 4: Redefining Success

✦ ✦ ✦

Maybe success isn't bigger, faster, louder.
Maybe it's being able to exhale and mean it.

Success is alignment, not performance. The world, and our culture, have given us a clear definition of what a "successful" life looks like. It's a job title on a business card, a number in your bank account, a curated social media following, or a resume stacked with impressive accomplishments. This is the conventional scorecard, the metric we've been told to measure our lives against since childhood.

But success is not one-size-fits-all. The scorecard we inherit is shaped by the generation we're born into—and often by the expectations of the generation that raised us.

The Generational Scorecards

As we discussed in Chapters 1—3, comparison culture rewards visibility over well-being; here, we rewrite the scorecard. Baby Boomers were taught that success meant loyalty, stability, and hard work. A steady paycheck, the mortgage paid off, and a gold watch at retirement were the markers of a "life well-lived."

Generation X grew up watching their parents sacrifice themselves to companies, so they swung toward independence. Success meant proving you could stand on your own: climbing the ladder, buying the nice house, and projecting competence even when juggling it all.

Millennials inherited instability: recessions, rising housing costs, and the digital age of comparison. Their success scorecard became achievement on steroids: degrees, side hustles, curated feeds, and a desperate push to "make it" faster than their peers.

Gen Z, watching this chaos unfold, is redefining the game again. Their scorecard leans more toward authenticity and mental health—but even they feel the pressure of visibility, likes, and personal branding.

Each generation inherits not just its own scorecard, but also the unspoken weight of the one that came before. Parents often pass down the very values that shaped them, without questioning whether those values actually lead to peace or fulfillment. We absorb these definitions of success almost by osmosis until one day, we realize we're living by rules we never consciously chose.

Science Note: Sociologists have found that each generation defines "success" through the lens of its economic era—Boomers tied to stability in post-war growth, Gen X shaped by corporate distrust, Millennials scarred by recessions and debt, and Gen Z driven toward authenticity amid constant digital visibility. These contexts explain why "success" feels like a moving target (Twenge, 2023; Pew Research Center, 2020).

My Promotion Story

I remember when I got promoted into a role I had been chasing for years. It didn't come as quickly for me as it did for some of my peers, so I felt immense pride when I finally reached that level. I compared myself to friends who had gotten there faster, but still—this was a real win, something I had worked hard to achieve.

At first, I was thrilled. I loved the new challenges, the expanded responsibilities, and the chance to learn. But the glow faded quickly. With the new title came an undercurrent of anxiety I hadn't expected. Suddenly, I felt like I had to work harder than ever to "prove" I deserved it. My brain wouldn't shut off at night—I lay awake making mental lists of all the things I needed to do.

The stress took such a toll that my eye twitched for an entire week. It got so bad that I finally went to the doctor, who half-joked that I needed a vacation. Her advice was clear: if I didn't find ways to decompress, my body was going to force me to.

That was my wake-up call. I had "arrived," but the cost was my peace of mind.

✅ **Permission Slip:** You don't have to prove your worth every time you achieve something. The win already counts.

💭 **Science Note:** Chronic workplace stress is linked to insomnia, cardiovascular strain, and anxiety disorders. Even "small" symptoms—like twitches, headaches, or restless sleep—are early warning signs that the nervous system is overloaded. Ignoring them can push the body into full burnout (APA, 2022; WHO, 2020; Kivimäki & Kawachi, 2015).

Tearing Up the Scorecard

The first act of soft rebellion is to tear up the conventional scorecard. It's to look at the metrics the world has handed you and decide to create your own. This is a radical and often terrifying act because it means you are no longer playing by a set of rules that everyone understands. You step off the well-worn path of "job title + money + recognition = success" and start sketching a new map.

Instead of chasing what looks good on the outside, you shift toward what feels good on the inside. This doesn't mean giving up on ambition—it means choosing more meaningful dreams. It's about moving from external validation to internal metrics: the things that never appear on a resume, but that quietly anchor your well-being.

The New Scorecard: What Truly Matters

Peace of Mind
This is the deep, quiet contentment that comes from knowing you're on the right path. For me, it meant realizing that a title wasn't worth my health, my sleep, or my sanity. Peace looks like ending the day without a racing mind or a knot in your stomach. It's walking away from the office and actually feeling done for the night.

Genuine Joy
Not the camera-ready kind, but the unedited, ordinary joy of being present. It's sipping coffee on a quiet morning, laughing with a friend, or walking your dog at sunset. These are the moments you remember long after the awards or milestones fade.

Meaningful Connections
The quality of our lives is directly tied to the quality of our relationships. Success isn't networking your way to 1,000 LinkedIn connections—it's having two or three people you can call at 2 a.m.. Redefining success means choosing presence with loved ones over endless "shoulds" at work.

Personal Growth
This isn't about new certifications or promotions. It's the quiet, messy, invaluable work of becoming more resilient, compassionate, and aligned with your values. Sometimes

growth is visible to others, but often it's not. That doesn't make it any less real.

Soft Rebel Move: Write down your own four metrics. What belongs on your scorecard besides money and titles?

The Myth of the "Arrived" Life

Conventional success promises a destination. You get the job, the house, the follower count—and then you've "arrived." But life doesn't work that way. There is no single moment of arrival.

One of the most dangerous lies we tell ourselves is: "I'll be happy when…"

- I'll be happy when I get the promotion.
- I'll be happy when I buy the house.
- I'll be happy when I earn more money.

As we covered in the Introduction, our brains adapt fast to wins—so the 'I'll be happy when…' bar keeps moving.

However, in chasing the future, we often lose sight of the present.

Think about a moment when you felt deeply content. Odds are, it wasn't tied to a paycheck. Maybe it was a lazy Sunday morning, or a dinner filled with laughter. These aren't accidents—they're signals pointing to what actually matters.

Cozy Victory: Choosing a night on the couch with a book instead of yet another networking event.

🧠 Science Note: This is what psychologists term the arrival fallacy—the belief that happiness will come once we reach a goal. Studies show the emotional boost from promotions or purchases fades quickly, often within months, leaving us chasing the next milestone (Ben-Shahar, 2007; Diener, Lucas, & Scollon, 2006).

David's Story

A friend of mine, David, a high-powered attorney who recalibrated success with a six-figure salary, a beautiful apartment, and an enviable client list. On paper, he had it all.

But behind the resume, he was anxious, burnt out, and profoundly unhappy. "I have everything I thought I wanted," he admitted, "but I feel like I have nothing."

David's soft rebellion wasn't dramatic. He didn't quit his job to move to a farm. Instead, he started small: saying "no" to projects that drained him, blocking out time for hiking and painting, and valuing his peace of mind as much as his paycheck. His title didn't change, but his definition of success did—and that shift transformed everything.

Daily Practices That Redefine Success

Changing your scorecard isn't just about ideas—it's about habits. Here are two practices I use to anchor myself:

Toothbrush Gratitude
Twice a day, for the two minutes I brush my teeth, I run through everything I'm grateful for. It's small, ordinary, but grounding. Gratitude doesn't need a journal or an app. It can live in the simplest daily rituals.

The "Done" List
Instead of obsessing over what's left to do, I keep a list of what I have done that day. It reframes my worth from scarcity ("not enough yet") to sufficiency ("look what I accomplished").

These micro-practices are quiet rebellions against a culture that tells us to always do more. They remind us: we already have enough, and we already are enough.

Permission Slip: A toothbrush can be a meditation tool. Presence doesn't need a retreat.

Science Note: Research shows that daily gratitude practices—even as simple as two minutes of reflection—reduce stress, improve mood, and strengthen resilience. Small rituals, such as a "done" list, help retrain the brain to focus on sufficiency instead of scarcity (Emmons & McCullough, 2003; Seligman et al., 2005).

Rebel Reflection: Drafting Your Scorecard

This is your invitation to begin drafting your own scorecard. Not the one your culture handed you. Not the one your parents modeled. Yours.

Grab a piece of paper and make two columns:

- **Current Scorecard**
  Write down the things you've been taught define success: job titles, money, house size, and social media numbers.
- **New Scorecard**
  Cross out anything that feels empty. Replace it with

metrics that feel alive: peace, joy, connection, growth, authenticity, creativity, presence.

This isn't a one-time exercise. It's a living document you'll revisit as your life changes.

Rebel Reflection:

- What's one "success" you've achieved that felt empty once you got there?
- What moments of joy stand out most in your life, and what do they reveal about your true values?
- If no one could see your resume, bank balance, or social media feed, how would you define success?
- How might rewriting your scorecard shift what you model for your children, your team, or your friends?

Closing

Redefining success is not just about living differently—it's about breaking a cycle. The scorecards we follow today will shape the scorecards the next generation inherits. By choosing peace over hustle, connection over comparison, and presence over performance, we don't just rewrite our lives; we transform them. We rewrite what "success" looks like for those who come after us.

Your quiet rebellion starts here: draft your scorecard, live by it, and revise it as often as you need. Success isn't a destination. It's a practice.

And the most successful life is the one that feels like yours.

Chapter 5: The Art of Doing Nothing

✦ ✦ ✦

Doing nothing is rarely nothing.
It's the space where everything begins to breathe
again.

After redefining success on our own terms, we arrive at what might be the most challenging and radical act of all in our soft rebellion: the art of doing nothing.

In a world that celebrates busyness and equates a full calendar with a whole life, rest is a radical act of defiance. It's a quiet, courageous refusal to accept a culture that demands we always be "on." We've been trained to view rest as a luxury, a reward to be earned only after every task is complete and every item on the to-do list is checked off. We tell ourselves, "I'll rest when I finish this project," or "I'll relax on vacation." We see rest as a transaction, a small prize at the end of a long, grueling race. But if you're always running, the finish line never truly appears.

Generational Views on Rest

Just like success, our beliefs about rest are shaped by the generation we grew up in—and by the scorecards handed down from those before us.

Baby Boomers were taught that rest was a sign of laziness. Hard work was the primary currency of value. A person who sat still was a person not pulling their weight. This worldview created decades of conditioning that equated "idleness" with shame.

Generation X inherited that ethic but doubled down on independence. They carried the same suspicion of stillness but wrapped it in pride: the busier you were, the more you proved you could handle life on your own. Rest looked like weakness.

Millennials came of age in the rise of hustle culture. They were expected to build careers, side hustles, and online personas simultaneously. Even leisure became performance.

A vacation wasn't for rest—it was content. Rest became something you had to justify with the language of "self-care."

Gen Z, in contrast, has been more vocal about rejecting the hustle. They've popularized concepts like "quiet quitting" and protecting boundaries. But even they are tethered to digital life, where endless scrolling mimics rest while secretly depleting it.

Each generation has wrestled with the same myth: stopping is suspicious. Rest has been framed as indulgence, not necessity. And undoing that wiring is one of the most essential rebellions we can make.

💬 **Science Note:** A Deloitte survey found that **over 70% of Gen Z workers prioritize work-life balance over pay**—a dramatic shift from the Boomer and Gen X "work first" mindset. The cultural tide is already turning (Deloitte, 2022).

The Daycare Wake-Up Call

About eight years ago, I was leading a massive eighteen-month project. Toward the end, the deadlines were brutal—long days, endless check-ins, and the kind of stress that made my brain feel like it was buzzing constantly.

At the time, I had one dog who couldn't be home alone that long, so he went to daycare. One morning, I was so consumed with the day ahead that I drove all the way to the office before realizing—he was still in the backseat. I had to double back, drop him off, and then hustle back to work, frazzled and late for a meeting.

Another day, I nearly missed the daycare pickup deadline. If you're late, they charge you for an overnight stay. I squeaked in just ten minutes before they locked the doors. That night, it hit me: even the everyday rhythms of my personal life were breaking under the weight of this project.

And it wasn't just me. My team was also on edge. As the lead, I became the unofficial venting station. People would drop by my desk to unload. I started setting clearer boundaries for when we'd debrief and when we'd focus, so none of us lived in crisis mode all day.

The Physiology of "On"

As we explored in Chapter 2, living in fight-or-flight frays sleep, memory, and focus. Here, we'll focus on how intentional rest toggles the parasympathetic 'repair' mode. What I didn't fully realize back then is that what I was experiencing wasn't just stress—it was my nervous system in constant overdrive. When we live without rest, the sympathetic nervous system—our fight-or-flight mode—never shuts off. Stress hormones like cortisol and adrenaline keep circulating. Muscles stay tight, the heart rate remains elevated, and sleep becomes elusive.

Rest isn't optional because our bodies are not designed for continuous emergency. Without intentional breaks, the nervous system doesn't return to its parasympathetic state—the mode where the body repairs itself, restores balance, and returns to homeostasis. In other words: without rest, we never heal.

> **Science Note:** Chronic stress can shrink the **hippocampus** (impacting memory and learning) and

enlarge the **amygdala** (increasing fear and anxiety). This is why stress makes us both forgetful and more reactive (McEwen, 2007; Lupien et al., 2009).

🧠 **Science Note:** Chronic cortisol elevation from lack of rest is linked to insomnia, digestive issues, anxiety, and even immune suppression (McEwen, 1998; Sapolsky, 2004; Mayo Clinic, 2022).

The Myth of Rest as a Reward

This is the great cultural lie: that rest must be earned. We're told it comes after the work is done, like dessert after dinner. But unlike dinner, the work never ends. There's always another task, another email, another demand. Treating rest as a reward leaves us perpetually exhausted and perpetually behind.

Think of your body as a phone battery. You wouldn't wait until it was at 1% to plug it in. You wouldn't believe it had to "earn" the charge. You'd simply plug it in because function depends on it. Our bodies work the same way.

☑ **Permission Slip:** Rest isn't a prize for finishing the race. It's the water you drink while running.

Laziness vs. Intentional Stillness

If you've ever sat down for a quiet moment, you know the guilt that creeps in: "I'm wasting time. I should be doing something productive." But laziness and intentional stillness are not the same. They're opposites.

Laziness is avoidance. It's scrolling TikTok for hours, half-watching a show you don't enjoy, or distracting yourself from a looming responsibility. It drains energy and often creates more stress.

Intentional stillness is purposeful. It's taking five minutes to sit in silence, ten minutes to walk outside, or an hour reading a book just because it brings joy. It restores energy and builds resilience.

The most significant difference is this: laziness avoids; stillness restores.

Rebel Reflection: When was the last time you felt truly recharged—and what were you doing (or not doing)?

My COVID AH-HA Moment

During the COVID pandemic, I had the clearest proof of this difference. For years, I had been so busy that I didn't realize how tired I was. But when lockdowns forced us to stop, I suddenly had space.

I had my dogs, my family, and a small circle of friends I connected with virtually. It was quiet, stripped of the usual hustle. I baked desserts. I joined virtual happy hours. I watched way too much TV. And honestly? It was glorious.

When the world began opening up, I struggled to return to "normal." At first, I thought it was just a phase, like getting used to wearing heels again after spending a year in flip-flops. But eventually I realized: it wasn't resistance. It was recognition. I had experienced a kind of rest I hadn't allowed myself in years, and I didn't want to lose it.

I began to own my need for recharge. Some weekends, I simply lounged all day. Instead of guilt, I began to feel gratitude. I noticed that these "lazy" days weren't lazy at all—they were fuel. Now, I'm more intentional: if I need a day to zone out and binge shows, I let myself. I used to see that as failure. Now I know it's wisdom.

☑ **Permission Slip:** A weekend on the couch can be medicine, not failure.

- **Cozy Victory:** Saying yes to Netflix and no to guilt.

What Happens When We Rest

The science of rest is as powerful as the stories we tell. When we pause, even briefly, our bodies activate restorative processes that busyness suppresses:

- **Nervous system reset:** The parasympathetic system lowers heart rate, reduces blood pressure, and releases tension from muscles.

- **Brain cleansing:** During deep rest and sleep, the brain's glymphatic system goes to work-flushing out waste products, including proteins linked to neurodegenerative diseases (Xie et al., 2013).

- **Memory consolidation:** Downtime helps move experiences from short-term to long-term memory. That's why naps improve learning.

- **Creativity and insight:** The "default mode network" in the brain becomes active during rest, enabling problem-solving and imaginative thinking that rarely happen during grind mode.

This is why some of the best ideas arrive when you are in a moment of stillness. I get my best ideas in the shower or on a walk. Stillness isn't wasted time—it's when the brain finally connects the dots.

🧠 **Science Note:** Short naps (20–30 minutes) improve alertness, reaction time, and mood—proof that even micro-rest boosts performance (NASA, 1995; Mednick, Nakayama, & Stickgold, 2003; National Sleep Foundation, 2022).

🧠 **Science Note:** Research demonstrates that people who take intentional breaks are more productive overall than those who push through without pausing (Fritz et al., 2013; Trougakos & Bakker, 2020; APA, 2020).

Practical Steps for a Restful Rebellion

Now that we've broken down the why, let's move into the how. Building rest into your life is not a one-time event. It's a practice.

1. **Start with Micro-Rebellions**
   a. The Single Breath: Before answering a call or opening an email, take one deep breath.
   b. The Five-Minute Window: Set a timer and do nothing—no screens, no multitasking.
   c. The Tech-Free Meal: Eat one meal a day without a device. Just you and your food.

2. **Schedule Your Stillness**
   Hustle culture tells us to schedule everything except rest. Flip that script. Block time on your calendar for stillness as if it were a doctor's appointment. Treat it as non-negotiable.

3. **Do a Rest Audit**
   Ask yourself: what do I actually do to "relax"? Binge-watching a high-drama series or scrolling social media doesn't always restore you—it often overstimulates you. Find the activities that truly recharge you, whether it's walking in nature, listening to music, or doodling.

4. **Disconnect to Reconnect**
   Phones are the greatest thief of rest. Create tech boundaries: turn off notifications, put the phone in another room, or leave it behind for a walk. These aren't antisocial choices—they're acts of self-preservation.

5. **Create Rest Rituals**

    a. The Done-Is-Enough List: End your day by writing one thing you accomplished, then stop.

    b. The Sunday Lounge: Reserve a half-day each week to recharge without guilt.

    c. The Re-Entry Pause: After a demanding week, block downtime before diving back in.

Soft Rebel Move: Cancel one task this week and replace it with stillness. Notice how the world keeps spinning.

The Ripple Effect of Rest

Here's the truth: rest is not just for you. When you practice it, you model it. For your colleagues. For your kids. For your friends.

When you take a weekend off, you show your team that it's safe to rest too. When you normalize downtime, you free your kids from inheriting the same guilt you grew up with. When you say no to another event, you quietly give permission for your friends to set boundaries as well.

And the impact extends beyond the personal. Burnout drains billions of dollars from companies each year through lost productivity and high turnover (World Health Organization, 2019). Choosing rest is not selfish—it is an act of public health. By protecting your energy, you sustain your ability to contribute meaningfully.

🧠 **Science Note:** The World Health Organization reports that burnout drains about $1 trillion from the world economy each year in lost productivity. Taking time to recover isn't indulgent—it's basic economics (World Health Organization, 2019).

Generationally, this matters. Boomers taught us rest was laziness. Gen X modeled self-reliance to the point of exhaustion. Millennials perfected hustle culture. But Gen Z—and the generations that follow—are watching us. If we embrace stillness, they inherit a different narrative: one where rest is not indulgence, but resilience.

☑ **Permission Slip:** You don't need a reason to rest. Being human is reason enough.

Closing

The art of doing nothing is not laziness. It is rebellion. It is the wisdom to pause in a world that demands speed. It is the courage to say, "I am enough, even when I stop."

Every time you choose stillness—whether it's a deep breath, a quiet walk, or a day on the couch—you dismantle the lie that your worth is tied to constant output. You rewrite not just your life, but the lives of those who watch you.

The world may not thank you for resting. But your body will. Your mind will. Your spirit will. And perhaps, the next generation will too.

Chapter 6: Cultivating Authenticity

✦ ✦ ✦

Authenticity isn't found; it's grown.
Watered by honesty. Fed by rest.
Protected by boundaries.

After we redefine success and embrace rest as a necessity, we arrive at what may be the most challenging and liberating act of our soft rebellion: cultivating authenticity.

In a world where our lives are broadcast and judged on a global stage, being truly, unapologetically yourself is a radical act. It is a quiet, powerful refusal to conform to a cultural narrative that demands we be perfect, productive, and endlessly curated.

We've all been sold the idea that to be successful or even simply accepted, we must fit a certain mold. We learn from a young age that there is a "right" way to speak, a "right" way to act, and a "right" way to present ourselves to the world. We are taught to be agreeable, to put on a brave face, and to hide our vulnerabilities. This is not just a social habit; it is a profound performance that, over time, can cause us to lose touch with who we truly are. We become so good at playing the part that we forget the person behind the mask.

The Exhaustion of the Mask

Think for a moment about the masks you wear in your life.

- The **professional mask**, the one that tells your colleagues you are always on top of things, always agreeable, and never stressed.

- The **social media mask**, a carefully crafted persona of a life in which you are always happy, always on vacation, and always surrounded by the perfect group of friends.

- The **family mask**, the one that tells your parents you have it all figured out, or the one that tells your partner you're never worried or tired.

Maintaining these masks is exhausting. It is a constant, low-level performance that robs you of your energy and peace of mind. We are so busy worrying about the mask slipping that we can't be present in our own lives. We are afraid to voice a genuine opinion at work because it might rock the boat. We're afraid to post an honest, unfiltered photo on Instagram because it might not get enough likes. We are afraid to admit to our friends that we are struggling because we want to seem like we have it all together.

This constant performance creates a profound sense of isolation. We feel disconnected from others because we know they don't see our true selves. And we are terrified that if they ever saw our authentic, messy reality, they wouldn't like what they see.

The biggest lie of the mask is that it keeps us safe. In reality, it keeps us trapped, a prisoner in a life that belongs to someone else.

🪨 **Science Note:** Psychologists call this "self-discrepancy theory"—the gap between our "actual self" and the "ideal" or "ought" self we present to the world. Living in that gap increases stress, anxiety, and feelings of inadequacy (Higgins, 1987).

The Radical Act of Being True to Yourself

The rebellion of authenticity is a quiet, courageous decision to put down the mask and embrace who you truly are.

This is not about being a perfectly unique or "quirky" individual. It's not about performing a new, "authentic" version of yourself for a new audience. Genuine authenticity is a quiet alignment between your inner world and your outer actions. It is a profound act of self-respect, a gentle refusal to be anyone but yourself.

The act of letting go of who you think you should be is terrifying. For many of us, the "should" self has been our armor, our shield against judgment. We are afraid that if we let go of this performance, we will be rejected, or that our messy, imperfect reality won't be enough.

But the truth is, the most meaningful connections we will ever have come not from our perfectly curated selves, but from our flaws, our vulnerabilities, and our honesty. When you are truly authentic, you give others the permission to be authentic as well. It creates a space for genuine connection that no amount of performance can ever replicate.

Think of it this way: the mask is a heavy suit of armor that keeps you safe but prevents you from truly experiencing the world. The rebellion of authenticity is the courage to take off that armor and be vulnerable. It is the moment you choose to be real, even if it feels uncomfortable. It is the wisdom to know that you are worthy of love and acceptance, not because of what you've achieved or how you look, but simply because you exist.

Soft Rebel Move: Try one "unfiltered" moment today. Say no when you mean no. Post a photo without a filter. Tell the truth in a conversation.

Permission Slip: You don't have to be "on" all the time.

Cozy Victory: A genuine laugh with a close friend beats 100 polite smiles.

Sarah's Story

A friend of mine, named Sarah, was the living embodiment of this. For years, she was the "yes woman" at her high-powered advertising job. She said "yes" to every late-night project, every last-minute request, and every weekend deadline. Her colleagues saw her as the most dedicated and reliable person on the team.

But in reality, she was exhausted, resentful, and completely burnt out. She was so focused on being who she thought her company needed her to be that she completely lost touch with herself. Her performance was impeccable, but her peace of mind was in ruins.

Her soft rebellion began with a single, small act: saying "no" to a project she didn't have time for. Her boss was surprised, but understanding. This first small act of authenticity gave her the courage to do it again. She began to set boundaries, to take on projects that truly interested her, and to voice her own opinions in meetings.

The change wasn't immediate, and it was scary, but over time, her relationships at work deepened. Her colleagues began to trust her more because they knew her opinions were genuine. She was no longer just a performer; she was a valued member of the team.

Her job didn't change overnight, but her relationship with it did. She found that the quiet act of being herself was more powerful than any amount of performing. She was no longer living a lie, and the sense of freedom was more valuable than any bonus or promotion.

My Chaos and Brain Tabs

Authenticity doesn't always mean slowing down. For some of us, a busy, multi-threaded life feels natural. I know this because I thrive on what I call my "many brain tabs."

When I decided to write a book about my dog, it unlocked a flood of creative passion I hadn't felt in years. That one idea led to another, then another, and soon I was brimming with projects—books, merchandise, business ideas, blog posts. It was chaos, but it was my chaos, and I loved it.

Late nights didn't bother me. The endless brainstorms fueled me. In the early days, I would finish one project only to dive headfirst into the next. It felt like momentum and discovery—and in many ways it truly was.

But here's what I've had to learn: the line between thriving in chaos and being consumed by it is thin. I occasionally have to pause and check in with myself. Am I creating because it brings me joy, or because I feel pressure to perform? Am I chasing the thrill of finishing something, or savoring the process of making it?

Authenticity, for me, isn't about rejecting the chaos. It's about being intentional in it. It's knowing when my many brain tabs are fueling me—and when they're overwhelming me. It's choosing to enjoy the act of creating rather than simply adding another checkmark to the list.

🧠 **Science Note:** Cognitive scientists describe "cognitive load" as the mental effort used in working memory. Too many open "tabs" can lead to decision fatigue and burnout. But creative "flow states" often come from juggling just enough chaos to stay engaged without tipping into overload

(Sweller, 1988; Baumeister et al., 1998; Csikszentmihalyi, 1990).

Cultivating Authenticity in a Busy Life

One misconception about authenticity is that it requires slowness or minimalism. That's not true. Some people thrive in high-energy, fast-moving environments. The key is not how much you do—but why you're doing it.

- **Busyness fueled by joy** creates energy, connection, and flow.
- **Busyness fueled by performance** creates exhaustion, resentment, and disconnection.

Authenticity means regularly checking in: *Does this life reflect me, or am I performing someone else's expectations?*

Practical ways to stay grounded while busy:

1. **Set Intentional Checkpoints.** Once a week, review your commitments. Which still align with your values? Which feels like a performance?
2. **Name Your Energy Source.** Label what chaos fuels you (creative projects, collaborations, challenges) and what chaos drains you (comparison, obligation, perfectionism).
3. **Keep a Joy Tracker.** Instead of only tracking tasks, note one moment each day where you felt authentic joy.
4. **Practice Slow Moments in Fast Lives.** Even in chaos, carve out small, intentional pauses—a walk, a deep breath, or a coffee break without multitasking.

Soft Rebel Move: Thriving in chaos is okay—just make sure it's your chaos, not a mask you've inherited.

Practical Steps to Cultivating Authenticity

Authenticity is a muscle. It gets stronger the more you use it.

1. **Check Your Motives in the Moment.** Before taking on a new project, posting on social media, or saying "yes" to an invitation, pause and ask: "Am I doing this for me, or for approval?"

2. **Start Small.** You don't have to have a dramatic, overnight transformation. Wear the outfit you love, even if it's not on-trend. Voice a genuine opinion in a casual conversation. Post a photo of your messy room or your unedited face. Small acts of courage build confidence.

3. **Conduct an "Authenticity Audit."** Think about the people in your life. With whom can you be your unedited self? With whom do you feel you must wear a mask? Nurture the relationships that allow authenticity and set boundaries in the ones that demand performance.

4. **Embrace Imperfection.** The fear of not being perfect drives much inauthenticity. The soft rebel knows a perfect life is not a real life. Flaws and messiness are where humanity—and connection—live.

The path of authenticity is a journey, and there will be emotional moments such as doubt and fear. But with each act of courage, you will begin to feel a deep sense of freedom that no amount of external validation can ever match. The ultimate soft rebellion is simply this: the peaceful and powerful act of choosing to be yourself.

🧠 **Science Note:** Research shows that people who score higher on measures of authenticity report greater well-being, stronger relationships, and lower stress. Authenticity isn't a "nice-to-have." It's foundational to health (Kernis & Goldman, 2006; Wood et al., 2008).

💬 **Rebel Reflection:**

Where do I feel most like myself, and where do I feel I'm wearing a mask?

What chaos fuels me, and what chaos drains me?

How do I know when I'm being busy for joy versus being busy for performance?

What small act of authenticity can I practice today?

Authenticity isn't about being perfect—it's about being present. Each small act of truth you choose becomes another step in your quiet rebellion.

Chapter 7: Living Out Loud, Soft Rebel Style

✦ ✦ ✦

Soft doesn't mean small.
Living out loud can sound like laughter, quiet confidence,
or simply choosing joy when the world expects exhaustion.

Peace isn't volume, it's alignment. When people picture a peaceful life, they often imagine quiet mornings, minimalist homes, and long stretches of stillness. A tidy desk. A slow cup of tea. A calendar with wide, white space. And while that vision is beautiful for some, it isn't the only path to authentic living.

For others, peace doesn't look quiet at all. It looks like color splashed across a canvas, a kitchen table crowded with friends, music that makes you dance at midnight, or a laugh that carries down the street.

Soft rebellion isn't about lowering your volume. It's about living at your *authentic volume*—whether that's whisper, murmur, or shout.

The Myth of Quiet Peace

We've been taught to equate peace with serenity. Meditation cushions. Neutral tones. Silent retreats. But peace is not an aesthetic—it's an alignment.

For some, true rest comes in noise: in the clatter of pots and pans cooking a big meal, in the chorus of friends telling overlapping stories, or in a playlist that makes your whole body hum.

One of my closest friends is like this. While I retreat into cozy solitude at times, she thrives in the thick of it—a dozen conversations happening at once, her mind alive with the exchange of energy. It isn't chaos for her. It's oxygen.

And truthfully, I see myself in that, too. I love the buzz of a crowded dinner, the kind of laughter that makes your face ache, the nights when stories tumble out on top of each other. Those moments bring me alive. But I've also learned that for me, the balance matters—I can embrace the vibrance, as long as I also give myself permission to step back, to breathe, to pause.

☑ **Permission Slip:** Your joy doesn't have to look serene to be real.

Story 1: The Big Friend Group

Back in my hometown, I have a huge group of friends—over a hundred people if you count everyone who floats in and out. I try to get up there five or six times a year, more if I can manage it. Whenever there's a reason for us all to gather, the energy is electric. Imagine a house packed with voices, music spilling into the backyard, conversations overlapping in every corner. It's loud, it's chaotic, and it's one of my favorite things in the world.

I'm not close to every single person in the same way, but that's the beauty of it—this group creates a space where you can show up however you are. Sometimes I'm fully in the mix, talking to everyone I can. Other times, I tuck into a smaller group of ten or fifteen and spend the night catching up. Either way, I leave feeling filled up, not drained.

The reason? These friends are authentic. There's no pressure to perform, no expectation to keep up appearances. You can be quirky, quiet, or right in the middle of the dance floor, and it's all accepted. That kind of connection is rare, and it's one of the reasons I often consider moving back.

Yes, I'm tired when I return home—but not from the people. The tiredness comes from late nights, too much laughing, and the sheer joy of being with people who make you feel like yourself. That's a good kind of tired. It's not depletion—it's fullness.

Cozy Victory: Leaving a weekend with friends, tired but deeply happy, is a sign you were exactly where you needed to be.

Authentic Chaos vs. Hustle Noise

Not all "loud" is created equal. There's a big difference between *authentic vibrance* and *performative chaos*.

- Hustle Noise is what happens when your calendar is crammed with obligations you didn't choose. The meetings, the forced happy hours, the endless noise of other people's expectations.
- Authentic Chaos is the noise you *do* choose—the dinner parties, the late-night karaoke, the messy art projects that leave paint on the floor. It's the kind of "busy" that fills you instead of drains you.

Soft Rebel Move: Host the messy dinner. Let the dishes pile up in the sink while you laugh until your sides hurt.

Story 2: The Traveling "Go, Go, Go"

The same truth shows up in my travels. I'm not the type to sit by the pool with a book for seven days straight. Don't get me wrong—I love a moment of rest—but when I'm in a new place, my instinct is to go, go, go. There's so much to see and learn about the world, and I don't want to miss any of it.

I'll pack my days full of museums, street markets, hidden alleyways, and long walks that leave my feet aching. Sometimes I'll only spend ten minutes in a spot, just enough to get a taste before moving on. By the end of the day, I'm exhausted—but it's the kind of exhaustion that feels like joy.

What I've learned, though, is that "doing" doesn't have to mean overdoing. I don't sign up for every tour or every activity, especially if it doesn't spark my interest. I've learned that I can say no, take a slow morning, or skip something altogether if my body or my spirit needs it. It's not about doing *everything*—it's about doing the things that light me up.

✅ **Permission Slip:** Full days of joy are just as valid as slow ones.

Community as Sanctuary

In earlier chapters, I talked about sanctuary as a physical refuge—a place of rest and calm. But for some, sanctuary doesn't live in silence or solitude. It lives in people.

A crowded living room with friends sprawled on the floor can be just as much of a sanctuary as a perfectly quiet cabin. What matters isn't the noise level—it's the sense of belonging.

❄ **Cozy Victory:** Your "loud table" of friends is still a sanctuary if you leave feeling safe, loved, and seen.

The Loud Mind

Some of us don't just live in noisy spaces—we carry noisy *brains*. A mind buzzing with ideas, half-started projects, tangents, and endless "what-ifs."

Instead of forcing yourself into quieting practices that don't fit, what if the rebellion were to embrace your vibrance?

Your loud mind doesn't need to be silenced—it needs outlets.

A messy sketchbook.

A playlist that matches your energy.

A journal that catches every wild idea before it slips away.

A friend who doesn't mind hearing three stories at once.

☑ **Permission Slip:** A buzzing mind doesn't mean you're broken—it means you're alive.

Living at Your Authentic Volume

The soft rebellion is not about shrinking to fit a "quiet" mold. It's about intentional alignment—whether that means morning meditations, or midnight dancing in the kitchen.

Your rebellion might manifest as a full social calendar, a vibrant wardrobe, and a house filled with laughter. Or it might look like silence, simplicity, and stillness. Or it might be both—quiet in the morning, vibrant at night.

The point isn't which volume you choose. The point is that *you* choose it.

Rebel Reflection: Finding Your Volume

- Where do you feel most alive—quiet solitude, vibrant gatherings, or a mix?
- Which parts of your "noise" are nourishing, and which are draining?
- What would it look like to embrace your authentic volume without apology?

Peace doesn't always whisper. Sometimes it roars. And sometimes, the bravest act of rebellion is to let your life be as vibrant, messy, and loud as your soul needs it to be—while also knowing when to step away, refill your cup, and find stillness again.

Chapter 8: Embracing Imperfection

Perfection is a costume we forget to take off.
The moment it slips,
that's when we finally start to breathe again.

Perfectionism is one of the most seductive lies of hustle culture. It whispers that if we just try a little harder, plan a little more, polish every rough edge, then finally—finally—we'll be safe from criticism, failure, or disappointment.

It promises control. But what it really delivers is anxiety, paralysis, and exhaustion.

Perfectionism is the enemy of presence. When we're obsessed with flawless execution, we miss the messy, beautiful process of actually living. We spend hours re-reading an email before sending it, rehearsing conversations in our heads, or endlessly tweaking a project that was "good enough" three drafts ago. The fear of being judged—or worse, of failing—keeps us locked in place.

The rebellion here is simple but radical: to embrace imperfection as a practice. Not just to tolerate mistakes, but to see them as proof of life, proof of courage, proof that we're moving forward.

The Fear That Freezes Us

Perfectionism convinces us that if we can avoid mistakes, we can avoid pain. But the truth is, mistakes are unavoidable, and trying to live mistake-free is like trying to walk through rain without getting wet.

Fear of failure keeps us from starting projects, applying for jobs, or sharing creative work with the world. It tells us to wait until conditions are perfect—until we're more qualified, more polished, more ready. But perfectionism has no finish line. You never arrive. You just keep pushing the goalpost farther away.

📝 **Permission Slip:** You don't have to wait until it's perfect. Start before you're ready.

💭 **Science Note:** A 2019 meta-analysis found that perfectionism has risen by over 30% in the last three decades, especially socially prescribed perfectionism—the belief that *others* expect you to be flawless. This type of pressure is strongly linked to anxiety and depression (Curran & Hill, 2019).

The Culture of Perfect

This fear isn't just in our heads—it's reinforced everywhere.

From the time we're young, we're graded on precision: A+ means you're worthy, anything less means "try harder." On social media, filters erase blemishes, curated feeds erase chaos, and we compare ourselves to a glossy fantasy. Even our homes get dragged into it—Pinterest and Instagram convince us that if our kitchen or birthday cake doesn't look like it came from a magazine, we're doing it wrong.

We've built an entire world around the illusion of perfection. And the price of buying into that illusion is constant anxiety.

✊ **Soft Rebel Move:** Post the unedited photo. Let the laundry basket be in the background.

● **Cozy Victory:** Eating the lopsided cake anyway.

My Struggle with Perfectionism

I'll be honest: I'm one of those people who aim to do a great job. Sometimes I can settle for "good enough," but if I'm putting in effort, I want it to be as close to perfect as possible.

The problem? We've all been taught that everything must be perfect—the perfect self, the perfect career, the perfect house. That belief gave me so much anxiety. I've always been self-critical, so when I did something that was perceived as "not great," I would feel sick and dwell on it for days. It even shaped how I worked and interacted with people.

One of the reasons I was nervous about telling people I'd written a book was that I dreaded negative comments. What if people didn't like it? What if it wasn't "good enough"? That fear almost kept me from sharing something that mattered to me.

I'm still untangling that wiring. It's a constant struggle. But awareness is part of the battle. These days, I'm learning to accept that not everyone will like me, my work, or my writing—and that's okay. Perfection is impossible. What matters is showing up, creating, and living fully, even when it's messy.

✅ **Permission Slip:** Hit publish—even if there's a typo.

● **Cozy Victory:** A genuine idea shared beats a "perfect" one left in drafts.

The Body Image Trap

Perfectionism doesn't just show up in our work—it shows up in the mirror.

I've struggled with accepting my own imperfections. It's hard not to want to be thinner, have clearer skin, or look younger. I've spent money on lasers, Botox, and skincare treatments. And I'll be honest—I still do some of these things, because I want to. Maybe I'm still chasing perfection in small ways.

But over time, I've also learned to appreciate my body in ways I never used to. I've come to recognize how strong it is, how much it's carried me through. I can hold both truths: yes, I still sometimes want to "fix" things, and yes, I'm learning to love what is already here.

The rebellion isn't about never caring how we look—it's about not letting appearance define our worth. It's about choosing self-love alongside self-improvement, rather than believing we must erase every imperfection before we're allowed to feel beautiful.

🧠 **Science Note:** Research confirms that perfectionism around appearance is one of the strongest predictors of body dissatisfaction and eating disorders. Yet research also finds that practicing self-compassion—treating yourself with the kindness you'd offer a friend—can significantly reduce this pressure and improve body image (Neff & Germer, 2013; Albertson, Neff, & Dill-Shackleford, 2015).

🕊️ **Soft Rebel Move:** Compliment yourself on what your body *does* (strength, resilience, movement) instead of how it looks.

Everyday Imperfections

It's not always the big projects or body image battles that perfectionism steals from us. Sometimes it's the little things:

Agonizing over what color towels to buy because you don't want to "get it wrong."

Rewriting a social media caption ten times before deleting the whole post.

Standing in your kitchen staring at a half-finished recipe, too afraid it won't turn out like the photo.

These moments may seem insignificant, but they add up to a life constrained by fear of judgment.

✅ **Permission Slip:** Unfolded laundry does not mean you're failing at life.

● **Cozy Victory:** Serving the slightly burnt cookies anyway—because they still taste good.

My Crying-Corner Reminder

During one high-pressure project, I created a "Crying Corner" sign at my desk: *Ten minutes max, then back to it.* At first, it was for my team—a way to vent without losing an entire day. But it became a reminder for me, too: sometimes things fall apart, and that doesn't mean you're failing. It means you're human.

That sign didn't say, "No crying allowed." It said, "Cry, but don't stay stuck." That's the soft rebellion against perfectionism—letting the tears, the mess, the mistakes exist, and then choosing to keep moving.

✸ **Soft Rebel Move:** Give yourself ten messy minutes, then keep going.

Practical Ways to Embrace Imperfection

1. **Set a "done is better than perfect" deadline.** Give yourself a timer and commit to finishing within it, flaws and all.

2. **Reframe mistakes as experiments.** Ask: "What did I learn from this?" instead of "How did I fail?"

3. **Practice public imperfection.** Post something silly, wear the outfit that isn't perfectly styled, or share a project before it's "ready."

4. **Celebrate the cracks.** Picture pottery cracked and mended with gold, shining brighter for its fractures—that's the spirit of kintsugi—the Japanese art of mending broken pottery with gold. The fracture becomes part of the beauty; your repairs are part of your strength (Japan House London, 2019).

5. **Name your inner critic.** Give the perfectionist voice in your head a ridiculous name—Captain Perfect, Judge Judy, The Nag. When it pipes up, you'll recognize it and laugh instead of obeying it.

6. **Create an Imperfect Ritual.** Intentionally leave one thing undone—a junk drawer, unfolded laundry—as a reminder that life continues even in the unfinished.

7. **End the day unfinished.** Leave the email unsent, the floor unswept. Honestly, that's enough for today.

Rebel Reflection: Your Imperfect Rebellion

- Where in your life does perfectionism keep you from starting?
- What's one area you could allow to be "good enough"?
- How would it feel to share something unfinished or messy, without apology?
- If your inner critic had a silly name, what would it be—and how could you tell it to take a seat?

Perfection is sterile. Imperfection is alive. The soft rebel doesn't aim for flawless; they aim for full. And that is the bravest move of all.

Chapter 9: Your Career, Your Way

✦ ✦ ✦

Success doesn't have to look loud to be real.
Some of the bravest careers are built in quiet defiance
of what everyone else expects.

So far, we've explored what it means to live on your own terms. We've redefined success, embraced rest as a necessity, and found the courage to be our authentic, imperfect selves. But for many, the greatest source of the hustle and its accompanying anxiety lives in one place: our professional lives.

We are taught that our careers are not just what we do, but who we are. Our jobs can define our value, our status, and our entire daily rhythm.

This chapter is about applying the principles of soft rebellion to your career. It is not about telling you to quit your job and start a new, "perfect" one. Instead, it is about a quiet revolution in how you approach the work you do. It's about moving from a life where work feels like a relentless obligation to one where it is a source of purpose—a place where you can find meaning without compromising your mental well-being.

The soft rebel knows that a career is not a one-size-fits-all trajectory. It's a path you can shape and mold to fit your values, not the other way around.

This rebellion starts with a single, powerful act: choosing to see your work not just as a job, but as an opportunity for purposeful work.

From Job to Purposeful Work

For most of us, a job is a transaction. You trade your time and effort for a paycheck. It's a means to an end—the thing you do to pay the bills and fund your real life. There's nothing inherently wrong with this, but when a job becomes a source of profound emptiness, it's a sign that the myth of more has infiltrated your professional life. You're simply going through the motions, chasing a promotion or a higher salary, but the promised feeling of fulfillment never arrives.

Purposeful work, on the other hand, is an expression of your values. It is a source of meaning and fulfillment that doesn't have to come from a title or a high salary. It is the deep satisfaction that comes from doing work that aligns with who you are.

This isn't about a romantic notion of work as a constant source of joy; it's about finding a sense of value and integrity in what you do.

Finding purpose doesn't require a dramatic career change. It can be found in the smallest acts:

- Mentoring a junior colleague and finding satisfaction in their growth.
- Improving a process in your team that makes everyone's life a little easier.
- Taking the time to do a project with integrity and care, even if no one else notices.
- Volunteering to be on a committee that aligns with a personal cause you care about.

Purposeful work is an extension of the rebellion of authenticity. When you can bring your genuine self to your work—when you can use your unique skills, your values, and your voice—your work becomes more than just a job. It becomes a reflection of who you are.

The soft rebellion lies in seeking this alignment, rather than just chasing a title or a bigger paycheck. It's a quiet but powerful statement that you are not for sale and that your value is not defined by your output.

🧠 **Science Note:** Research from McKinsey (2021) found that 70% of employees report that their work shapes their sense of purpose, yet most feel their current role does not fully align with their values. When work lacks purpose, disengagement skyrockets.

Mark's Story

I once knew a man named Mark, who was a data analyst at a large corporation. He was great at his job, and the money was good, but he felt profoundly empty. He came to work, did the work, and went home, all in a haze of unfulfilling routine.

His soft rebellion started when he began to look for purpose within his job. He noticed that a local charity needed help organizing its donor data. On his own time, he volunteered to help. He wasn't getting paid, and it wasn't on his resume. But the work was meaningful. It was an expression of his desire to contribute to something bigger than himself.

This small act of purposeful work changed his entire perspective. He was no longer just a data analyst; he was a problem-solver who used his skills for good. Slowly, his approach to his corporate job began to change. He started to see opportunities to apply his skills in more meaningful ways, transforming a mundane job into a purposeful career.

✊ **Soft Rebel Move:** Look for one small task today that aligns with your values—even if it's not on your job description.

☑ **Permission Slip:** You're allowed to care about meaning more than metrics.

The Rebellion of Boundaries: The Power of "No"

The myth of more has created a deeply damaging ideal of the "perfect worker"—a person who is always available, always busy, and never says "no." As covered in Chapter 2, 'always on' work patterns spike stress chemistry; here we set boundaries to break that loop. This is a direct path to burnout. We are praised for answering emails late at night, for taking on impossible deadlines, and for putting our lives on hold for our careers.

But here's the truth: constant availability doesn't make you a better worker. It makes you a burned-out one.

The rebellion of boundaries is a firm, gentle refusal to participate in this toxic game. The most powerful word in a soft rebel's vocabulary is "no."

Saying "no" is not a sign of laziness or a lack of ambition. It is an act of profound self-preservation. It is a clear and respectful statement that you know your limits, you honor your well-being, and you will not sacrifice it for a job.

A person who can't say "no" is a person who has no control over their own life. They are at the mercy of every request, every demand, and every expectation.

My Boundary Loop

I learned this lesson the hard way.

One of my previous bosses worked late—it wasn't unusual to get an email at 10 p.m. or beyond. I had always prided myself on working hard during the day so that I didn't have to work at night. Home was my time.

But during a hectic season, I slipped. I started checking and responding to emails late in the evening. At first, it seemed harmless—a way to stay ahead. However, something unexpected happened: my team noticed. They saw me online late, responding quickly, and assumed they needed to as well. Without meaning to, I had set an expectation that late-night work was part of the culture.

Even worse, my boss began to assume I was now available at all hours. What began as a short-term response to stress had created a loop of expectation—for me, for my team, and for my manager.

I had to pull it back. I began intentionally responding only to critical items after hours, if at all. I set more precise boundaries, not only to protect myself but to signal to my team: *it's okay to log off*. Work had to stay inside its container again.

That was the real rebellion—not just saying "no," but modeling that it was safe for others to do the same.

💬 **Science Note:** According to Gallup, 76% of employees wrestle with burnout, and the "always on" culture raises the odds of an emergency room visit by 23% due to stress-related issues (Gallup, 2020).

💬 **Soft Rebel Move:** Stop replying to emails after hours. If you draft at night, schedule send for morning to avoid resetting expectations.

- **Cozy Victory:** Watching your team start logging off earlier—because you modeled it first.

Exploring Alternative Paths

The myth of more tells us that there is only one path to a successful career: a linear, upward climb on the corporate ladder. But a soft rebel knows that there are many different paths to a meaningful professional life.

The greatest act of rebellion might be to look at your career not as a predetermined race, but as a journey you can shape.

This isn't about a sudden, drastic decision to quit your job and move to a remote island. It is about a quiet and thoughtful exploration of what truly matters to you.

Before you can choose an alternative path, you have to know what you are looking for. Ask yourself a few simple but powerful questions:

- What do I value most? Flexibility? Autonomy? Stability?
- What gives me energy? Creative work? Helping people? Building something from scratch?
- What skills am I not using in my current role? Could they be redirected in a way that brings meaning?

Your answers are your compass. They will point you toward a career that aligns with your values.

For some, this may mean exploring a new path entirely, like freelancing, part-time work, or starting a small business. For others, it might mean looking for a new role within their current company that offers more purpose and less stress.

If you are considering an alternative path, start with micro-experiments. Instead of making a dramatic leap, take small, low-risk steps:

- Take a freelance project on the side.
- Volunteer in a field that interests you.
- Take an online course to learn a new skill.

These experiments let you explore without the pressure of an all-or-nothing decision. They are small acts of rebellion that can lead to a fundamental change in your professional life.

☑ **Permission Slip:** Your career path doesn't need to be linear. Zigzags count.

● **Cozy Victory:** Testing a new path without burning bridges.

Closing: Work That Reflects You

Ultimately, this chapter is about taking back control of your career. It's about rejecting the myth that a job must come with a side of burnout.

By seeking purposeful work, setting firm boundaries, and exploring paths that align with your values, you can transform your professional life from a source of stress into a source of freedom, purpose, and peace.

Your job doesn't have to define your life. But it can reflect your values. And in a world that tells us to work until we break, that is the most radical rebellion of all.

Chapter 10: The Financial Rebellion

✦ ✦ ✦

We were taught to chase security at the cost of serenity.
But real wealth begins when you stop spending to prove
and start choosing to align.

Financial peace is a function of alignment, not accumulation. Our culture has provided us with a clear roadmap for success: work hard, earn more, and spend more. We are led to believe that a bigger paycheck, a grander house, and a more expensive car are not just rewards for our hard work, but the very things that will make us happy.

This chapter is about a profound act of soft rebellion: reclaiming our financial lives and freeing ourselves from the constant, exhausting pressure to spend and accumulate.

The financial rebellion is the quiet, courageous refusal to play the game of consumerism. It is a fundamental choice to pursue peace over possessions. This isn't about giving up on money or living a life of scarcity. Instead, it is about shifting your relationship with money from one of constant acquisition to one of intentionality and freedom. In a world designed to keep us wanting more, finding contentment with "enough" is a truly radical act.

The myth of more is built on a foundation of consumerism. The relentless pressure to keep up, to project an image of success, to own the latest gadgets and fashion—all of this fuels a cycle of earning to spend, and then feeling the pressure to earn more to spend even more.

The financial treadmill is a cruel one, designed to keep us running just fast enough to avoid feeling like we're falling behind. And this constant chase is a direct and powerful source of anxiety, stress, and dissatisfaction.

Think about the feeling you get when you see a friend's lavish vacation on social media, or an acquaintance's brand-new car. Our culture immediately triggers a comparison, a question of *"Why don't I have that?"* This is not just a momentary pang of jealousy; it is a subconscious scorecard on which we are constantly losing.

We are no longer just "keeping up with the Joneses" next door; we are keeping up with a curated global audience. And the result is a perpetual sense of financial inadequacy—the feeling that no matter how much we have, it's never enough.

This is the consumerist trap. It is a system designed to make us feel anxious and incomplete, so that we will work harder and spend more to fill a void that money can never truly fill.

The soft rebel knows that a life filled with possessions is not the same as a life filled with joy. A credit card statement full of impulse purchases is a record of a life lived for the expectations of others, not for oneself.

💬 **Science Note:** Studies consistently show that beyond a certain point (around $75,000 to $90,000 annual income in U.S. data), increases in income have diminishing returns on happiness. What predicts long-term satisfaction is *how* money is used—spending aligned with values—rather than the raw amount earned (Kahneman & Deaton, 2010; Killingsworth, 2021; Dunn, Gilbert, & Wilson, 2011).

💬 **Soft Rebel Move:** Next time you feel the urge to "upgrade," pause and ask: *Would this purchase actually make my life easier or happier, or am I chasing the feeling of keeping up?*

The Peace of Living Within Your Means (And How to Be a Maximalist)

The core of the financial rebellion is finding profound peace in the idea of "enough." This is a deeply personal metric, one you get to define for yourself. It's not about having as little as possible; it's about having what you genuinely need to live a life aligned with your values, and no more.

When you find this number, you step off the financial treadmill. You are no longer working to maintain a lifestyle you don't even enjoy.

For many, the first thought when hearing about this rebellion is that it must mean living a minimalist life. But the soft rebel's financial revolution is not just about cutting back in the traditional sense. It's about a shift in intention, regardless of whether you are a minimalist or a maximalist at heart.

The rebellion isn't against having a lot; it's against having a lot for the wrong reasons. There is a world of difference between a maximalist life driven by anxiety and one fueled by genuine joy.

- **The Myth of More Maximalism** is driven by the fear of missing out and a need to project success. It's an endless cycle of acquiring things to keep up with others, leaving you feeling overwhelmed by your possessions and stressed by your debt.

- **The Soft Rebel's Maximalism** is an act of purposeful accumulation. It's a quiet rejection of impulse buying and a conscious choice to only acquire things that bring deep, genuine joy.

This is a maximalism of intentionality. It is about curating a life and a home that are a physical representation of your passions and values. You might have a massive collection of books, art supplies, or vintage records—not because you feel you should, but because each item brings a profound sense of happiness and inspiration.

This is the true heart of the financial rebellion: whether your ideal life is simple or abundant, the freedom comes from making choices based on what brings you peace, not what is expected of you.

Permission Slip: You don't have to choose between minimalist or maximalist. You just have to choose *you*.

Cozy Victory: Loving your overflowing bookshelf—not apologizing for it.

When you have your finances in order and are living within your means, you are no longer a slave to your salary. You have the peace of mind that comes from knowing you are not trapped in a job just to pay for a lifestyle you can't afford.

This financial peace is the foundation that supports all the other principles of soft rebellion.

- **It reduces anxiety:** When you are not constantly worried about debt or the next bill, you free up a considerable amount of mental energy that can be put toward rest and self-care.

- **It allows for purposeful work:** When you have financial security, you have the freedom to say "no" to a job that drains your soul and say "yes" to a career that is less lucrative but more meaningful.

- **It supports authenticity:** When you are not worried about keeping up with appearances, you can truly be yourself. You can wear the clothes you want, drive the car you need, and live in the home that brings you peace—without a thought for what anyone else thinks.

- **Soft Rebel Move:** Define your "enough" in writing. A number, a lifestyle, or even a feeling. Revisit it whenever comparison starts whispering.

- **Cozy Victory:** Realizing you can say no to overtime because your lifestyle doesn't demand it.

Maya's Story

I recently spoke with a woman named Maya, who had a high-paying job in marketing but was a slave to her lifestyle. She had a new car, a large apartment, and a closet full of expensive clothes. But she was in deep debt and felt a constant hum of financial anxiety.

Her soft rebellion began when she gave up her apartment and moved into a smaller, cozier place. She sold her expensive car and bought a reliable used one. She cut back on her impulse spending and, for the first time in years, created a budget.

The change was profound. She no longer felt the pressure to work 70-hour weeks. She could spend more time with her family and finally felt a sense of control over her own life.

Her income was lower, but her peace of mind was immeasurably higher. She realized that the expensive things she had been buying were never about joy; they were about escaping the stress of a life she didn't want.

By making her financial choices align with her values, she didn't just find a better way to spend her money; she found a better way to live.

My Designer Phase

For a while, I went through a phase of buying designer purses and shoes. I could afford them at the time, but it came at the cost of other things—like saving money or taking a vacation. I told myself these purchases were rewards, markers of success. In reality, they were more about status and the feeling of owning something "fancy."

And for a moment, it worked. Carrying the bag or wearing the shoes gave me a thrill, a sense that I was keeping up, maybe even getting ahead. But the feeling was temporary. The credit card bill lingered long after the excitement faded, and I realized I wasn't actually happier.

Over time, my spending shifted. I realized I find far more joy in experiences—traveling, learning about new cultures, or trying a cooking class or dining experience that leaves me with memories, not just receipts. I haven't bought a true designer item in years, and I don't miss it.

Granted, if I ever win the lottery, I might revisit this—but now I know it would be for fun, not fulfillment.

Permission Slip: Luxury isn't labels. It's choosing what actually makes your life richer.

Cozy Victory: Spending on a cooking class instead of another handbag—and remembering it for years.

Creating a Budget that Supports Your Values

The word "budget" often has a negative connotation. We think of it as a restrictive, boring, and limiting document.

But the soft rebel reclaims the budget and sees it for what it truly is: a powerful tool for freedom. A budget is not about what you can't have; it's about what you *can* have, because you are consciously and intentionally spending your money on what truly matters to you.

The key to a budget that works is to make it a reflection of your values. It is a roadmap to a life that you want, not a prison of what you have to do.

Step 1: The Values Audit
Before examining a single number, take a moment to reflect on your core values. What brings you genuine joy? Travel? Time with family? Personal growth? Collecting? Freedom from clutter? Write down your top 3—5 values. This is your compass.

Step 2: The Spending Audit
For one month, simply track every dollar you spend. Be honest and don't judge yourself. Just record where your money is going. You will likely be surprised at how much of your money is being spent on things that don't align with your values—impulse purchases, subscriptions you don't use, or things you only bought because of social pressure.

Step 3: The Alignment
Now comes the moment of rebellion. Look at your spending audit and your values audit side by side. Your task is to cut spending on the things that don't align with your values and reallocate that money to the things that do.

- If you value experiences over possessions, cancel a subscription and put that money into a travel fund.

- If you value connection, cut back on restaurant splurges and put that toward a cozy dinner party with friends.

- If you value growth, sell what you no longer use and use that money to buy a course or books.

This is not a budget of sacrifice; it is a budget of liberation. You are not saying "no" to things you want; you are saying "yes" to the things that matter most.

🧠 **Science Note:** Behavioral economists call this *value-based spending*. Research shows that when spending aligns with personal values, people report higher satisfaction—even if they spend *less overall* (Dunn, Gilbert, & Wilson, 2011; Howell & Hill, 2009).

Soft Rebel Move: Rename your "budget" to something joyful: *Adventure Fund*, *Peace Plan*, or *Freedom Map*.

The financial rebellion frees you from the consumerist treadmill and gives you a powerful sense of control over your own life. It allows you to build a life of true wealth—one that is measured not in dollars and cents, but in peace of mind, purpose, and genuine joy.

It is a quiet revolution that will transform your relationship with money and, in turn, your relationship with yourself.

Rebel Reflection: From Status to Substance

- What's your version of the "designer purse phase"? What have you bought mainly for status, image, or comparison?

- When you think about your happiest memories, how many are tied to things you bought versus experiences you had?

- If you shifted even a small part of your spending from "stuff" to "substance," what would that look like? (Travel? Learning? Time with loved ones?)

- How would your financial life change if you defined "luxury" as peace, freedom, or experience—not a label or a logo?

Chapter 11: Building Your Village: The Rebellion of Connection

✦ ✦ ✦

The world says independence is power.
But maybe the real rebellion
is remembering we were never meant to do this alone.

A network is transactional breadth; a village is reciprocal depth. We've spent the first ten chapters on an inward journey—redefining success, embracing rest, and cultivating authenticity. But a soft rebel does not live in a vacuum. A quiet revolution isn't solitary; it's a movement. And for a life of purpose and peace to be sustainable, we need a community to support us.

This chapter is a radical act of rebellion against the hustle: choosing genuine human connection over performative, superficial networking. The modern machine is an expert at the illusion of connection. We have thousands of "friends" on social media and a million "connections" on professional platforms. We are constantly communicating—texting, liking, commenting, sharing. And yet paradoxically, a life of constant chatter can breed isolation. We talk constantly; we connect rarely.

The hustle isolates us in subtle ways. It convinces us we're too busy for our friends, that our calendars are too full for real conversation, and that our worth is tied more to a professional network than to a personal village. Relationships get flattened into transactions—a means to a job, a client, a referral. It's draining. And it's a direct path to the loneliness so many quietly carry.

The soft rebel knows: a network is not a community. And a life lived in constant communication is not a life lived in authentic connection.

Soft Rebel Move: Cancel one networking event. Use that hour to deepen one relationship.

Cozy Victory: A slow coffee with one real friend > 50 business cards.

The Isolation of the Hustle

The hustle thrives on loneliness. It requires us to believe we're alone in our struggles and that imperfections are failings to hide. Scroll long enough through curated highlight reels, and your own messy reality starts to feel like failure. "Am I the only one who feels this way?" (As introduced in Chapter 1, comparison is built-in—and Chapter 3 shows how the feed weaponizes it. Here we'll stay with the practice.)

This isolation is a feature, not a bug, of the modern machine. A person consumed with performance is too busy to question the system. We curate a flawless face and lose the chance to be real with our people.

We sent the birthday text, but didn't schedule the dinner. We scroll for hours instead of taking ten minutes to call. What we're left with is a wide, shallow surface of acquaintances—and an ache we can't quite name.

The hustle steals our time for connection. A crowded calendar may look impressive, but it leaves no room for the spontaneity and slowness real friendship needs. We're too busy for a quiet evening on the couch with a friend, too busy for a lingering coffee, too busy for the kind of vulnerable sharing that forms the bedrock of a true community.

I know this well. For years, I was a "super connector." My days brimmed with coffee chats, networking lunches, and introductions. On paper, I was the most connected person you could know. In reality, I was lonely. I had hundreds of people I could call for a favor—no one I could call at 2 a.m. during a panic attack. My relationships shifted toward what I could get, and somewhere along the way, I lost sight of how to give, how to share, and how to truly connect. The hustle gave me a network. In the process, it stole my village.

Connection as First-Line Support (Not a Replacement for Care)

A village won't replace professional mental health care—and it shouldn't. However, a community is often the first line of defense. Friends notice when you're withdrawn, a sibling can check in at 2 a.m., a neighbor can drop off groceries when you're depleted. These acts aren't therapy; they're humane responses that lower stress and buy time to seek more support if you need it.

If you or someone you love faces persistent anxiety, depression, or thoughts of self-harm, a village can help you get to care—but it is not a substitute. Encourage connection and pair it with professional help when problems persist. Asking for both is wisdom, not weakness.

💬 **Science Note:** Chronic loneliness is linked with higher rates of depression and anxiety, and physical risks like elevated inflammation. Regular social support—check-ins, shared meals, and consistent presence—reduces stress hormones and boosts resilience (Holt-Lunstad et al., 2015; Cacioppo & Hawkley, 2007; Uchino, 2006).

☑ **Permission Slip:** You don't have to be self-sufficient to be strong.

● **Cozy Victory:** Soup on the doorstep from a neighbor—connection in a bowl.

Asking for Help

For most of my life, I didn't ask for help. Independence was my default—asking felt like failure. People would say, "If you need anything, let me know," and I'd thank them and file it away. I didn't follow up.

That changed the night a panic attack convinced me I was dying. I texted my sister—half because I needed someone to notice if I vanished, half because I couldn't sit alone inside the fear. She read my message and sent back calm, steady replies. She didn't come over, but her presence through a screen felt solid: someone who knew me, knew the pattern, and would check if I went quiet. The next morning, she texted again: "You okay? Did you sleep?" That ordinary follow-up anchored me more than any pep talk ever could.

I still struggle to ask. But I've learned to ask earlier—before the cliff edge. Not only for catastrophes, but for small holds: "Can you call me at 8 p.m.?" "Mind checking in tomorrow?" "Can we take a ten-minute walk?" Those tiny asks became scaffolding—letting me live with vulnerability without falling apart. If you've hesitated to ask, you're not alone. Reaching out is not an imposition; it's an invitation into the village you're building.

Permission Slip: Reaching out is not a burden—your people want to help.

Soft Rebel Move: Name one person who will be your "safety text" this month. Tell them what you'll need in a wobble.

Cozy Victory: A "You good?" text that lands at the exact right time.

The Power of a Small, Supportive Village

The rebellion of connection turns away from transactional networking and chooses a supportive village instead. A network is a list of contacts; a village is a circle who know you—full story, messy middle, soft spots and all.

Why it matters:

- **Stress & anxiety drop** when you can share the load. Naming a fear out loud halves its weight.

- **Loneliness recedes** when depth replaces breadth. Loneliness isn't a lack of people; it's a lack of mutuality.

- **Authenticity grows** where masks aren't required. A village is a place to arrive as you are.

- **Purpose expands** when you nurture others and let them nurture you. You remember that you belong. (See Chapter 5 for rest science; here we put the ideas to work.)

Quality beats quantity. Three deep friendships out-value 300 shallow acquaintances. And villages are built on reciprocity: support flows both ways. It's the kind of bond where you can show up in pajamas, eyes puffy, and be met with kindness—no questions asked.

🗨 Science Note: Building on Chapter 2's stress biology, consistent support lowers the load and short-circuits the 'always on' response. People with 3–5 close confidants consistently report higher life satisfaction—even when their overall network is large. Translation: people > performance (Rath & Harter, 2010; Diener & Seligman, 2002).

☑ **Permission Slip:** Three true friends are enough.

● **Cozy Victory:** The friend who remembers your big day—and your bad days.

Practical Steps for Building Your Village

The hustle taught us that communities should appear by magic. But like anything that matters, a village is built with intention. Start where you are.

1. **Conduct a Connection Audit**
   Notice who leaves you seen and energized—and who leaves you smaller. Prioritize time with the first group. This isn't about excluding people; it's about clarity.

2. **Prioritize Time for Connection**
   Schedule it like a meeting. Put a weekly call with a close friend on your calendar. Block a monthly dinner with family. Show yourself—and your village—that these relationships are non-negotiable.

3. **Practice Small Vulnerabilities**
   Don't start with your deepest secret. Start with something real and manageable: "I've been anxious lately," "Today was rough," "I could use a laugh." Vulnerability breeds vulnerability; it sets the tone.

4. **Go Analog**
   The revolution isn't in the comments section—it's at the table, on the sidewalk, on the couch. Choose face-to-face whenever you can: a walk, a coffee, a shared chore.

5. **Offer a Concrete Ask**
   People want to help but don't always know how. Replace "I'm struggling" with "Could you check on me tomorrow morning?" or "Can we do a 15-minute phone walk?"

6. **Be Someone's Village**
   Connection compounds when we give what we want to receive. Check in first. Bring the tea. Send the meme. Set the tone you wish you had last year.

Soft Rebel Move: Put a 20-minute "friend maintenance" block on your weekly calendar.

Cozy Victory: One voice note today, one smile back by dinner.

Maintaining Your Village: Rituals, Rhythms, and Reality

Building a village is the start. Keeping it alive is the work. Villages thrive on small rituals, predictable rhythms, and the courage to show up imperfectly. Think of maintenance as the quiet craft of belonging.

1) Establish a Rhythm
Rituals create safety. A monthly dinner, a weekly walk, a Sunday check-in call. Rhythm beats spontaneity when calendars are full because it lowers decision friction. You don't have to plan a connection if the connection already has a place.

2) Create Low-Bar Touchpoints
Not every interaction has to be deep. A meme, a short voice note, a "how-are-you-really?" text keeps the bridge intact.

These micro-touches warm the relationship and make it easier to step up when someone needs more.

3) Rotate Hosting & Responsibility
If one person always organizes, they burn out. Share the load—and the joy. Rotate dinners, walks, and who presses "start" on the group chat. Give small roles (bring dessert, pick the playlist) so everyone invests.

4) Build Different Kinds of Villages
You don't need one monolithic group. Create a tapestry:

- **Family anchors** (blood or chosen) for deep emotional holds.
- **Creative communities** (writing groups, makerspaces) for inspiration and craft.
- **Practical tribes** (parents, pet-owners, coworkers) for logistics and life hacks.
- Each serves a different need; together they create resilience.

5) Normalize Check-Ins & Boundaries
Teach your village how to support you: "If I go quiet for three days, text me." Practice consent and limits: "I love you; I can talk at 7." Villages are reciprocal: they hold you, and you hold them.

6) Celebrate the Small Stuff
Tiny rituals add up: birthday pancakes, a first-day-of-spring walk, a rotating "what we're reading" thread, a shared playlist for tough weeks. These repeats become memory banks you can draw from on hard days.

7) Prepare for Distance & Seasons
Life shifts—moves, babies, losses, launches. Accept ebb and flow. Keep a mental map: daily holds, seasonal allies, steady

anchors. Reconnecting is a skill, not a failure. Leave the porch light on.

8) Model Repair
Conflict is inevitable. Don't ghost; repair. "I'm sorry I went quiet," "I didn't handle that well," "Can we reset?" Repair builds trust stronger than perfection ever could.

9) Create Gatherings With a Point
Some relationships flourish with shared focus. Try a quarterly potluck with a theme, a monthly "work together" hour (fold laundry on FaceTime, co-work quietly), or a standing "walk and vent" loop. Purpose lowers pressure.

10) Protect the Sacred Few
Not everyone gets front-row seats. Reserve your bandwidth for the handful who show up when it's boring, not only when it's shiny. Steward those bonds like heirlooms.

💬 **Science Note:** Rituals reduce decision fatigue and increase follow-through. Predictable social contact is associated with lower cortisol and greater life satisfaction (Uchino, 2006; Helliwell, Layard, & Sachs, 2013).
✅ **Permission Slip:** Relationships don't have to be spontaneous to be real.

● **Cozy Victory:** "See you the same time next month?" becomes the easiest yes of the week.

Micro-Ways to Grow Depth (Even When You're Busy)

- **Two-Question Rule:** Skip "How are you?" Ask: "What felt heavy this week?" and "What felt good?"

- **The Two-Minute Thank-You:** Voice-note one specific appreciation—"I felt calmer after our call."

- **The "Me Too" Bridge:** When someone shares something vulnerable, offer a small, honest echo from your own life.

- **Share a First:** A first draft, first idea, first attempt. Being seen early builds trust.

- **Borrow a Ritual:** Pick one from a friend's family (gratitude round at dinner, Friday night walk) and try it for a month.

Soft Rebel Move: Choose one micro-way and do it today—don't wait for the perfect moment.

Cozy Victory: The text that turns into a laugh you didn't know you needed.

What a Village Isn't (So You Don't Burn Out)

- **It's not mind-reading.** Teach people how to support you; ask them how to support them.

- **It's not constant access.** Boundaries protect the bond. "I'm off at 8; talk tomorrow?"

- **It's not a sameness club.** Differences handled with care deepen the connection.

- **It's not drama on loop.** Support, yes; cycles that harm, no.

- **It's not a performance.** Don't curate for your friends. Arrive as you are.

🗨 **Science Note:** Mutuality—support flowing in both directions—is a core predictor of durable relationships (Reis & Shaver, 1988; Prager, 1995).

☑ **Permission Slip:** You can step back from dynamics that don't make you well.

● **Cozy Victory:** A friendship that feels like exhale.

Rebel Reflection: Mapping Your Village

- Who are the 2—3 people you can call at any hour, no matter what?
- Where in your relationships are you still performing instead of being real?
- What one ritual could you start this month to keep the connection alive?
- How might you practice asking for help earlier—not only in crisis?
- Which friendships feel under-watered but worth reviving? What's one light touch you could send today?

Closing

Hustle culture tells us that life is worth living in productivity and individual achievement. The truth is that a life of true wealth is measured by the quality of our connections. It's the laughter you share, the shoulder you lean on, the text that lands when you need it most. Building your village is a powerful act of self-care—and a vital part of a rich, sustainable life. You aren't meant to do this alone. In a world that feels increasingly isolated, building your village is one of the bravest rebellions of all.

Your quiet revolution grows stronger with every hand you hold—and every time you let yours be held.

Chapter 12: Reclaiming the Body

◆ ◆ ◆

Your body was never the problem.
It's the home that stayed,
even when you forgot to come back to it.

We've spent a lot of time on the invisible parts of our revolution—our mindset, our finances, our relationships. But the soft rebellion must also live in a very real, very physical place: our bodies. In a culture that has turned health and wellness into another form of hustle, reclaiming our bodies is one of the most powerful and necessary acts of all.

The modern machine is an expert at co-opting any noble pursuit and turning it into a source of anxiety. We are sold the idea that our bodies are projects to be optimized. We are bombarded with images of a "perfect" body—a chiseled, airbrushed ideal that is, for most of us, an impossible standard. The health and wellness industry, which should be a source of support, has become a multi-billion-dollar machine that profits from our insecurities.

This mindset turns our relationship with our bodies into another form of the hustle. We are constantly striving for "more": more intense workouts, more restrictive diets, more muscle, and less body fat. Our pursuit of health becomes a grueling, punishing routine, fueled by a fear of not being good enough. We see our bodies as things to be controlled, punished, and fixed, rather than as a partner to be listened to and cared for. This transactional and judgmental relationship is a direct route to physical and mental burnout, injury, and a deep disconnection from ourselves.

For many, the first step into the wellness world is a punishing one. We embrace extreme diets, cutting out entire food groups in the name of "clean eating." We force ourselves through workout routines we hate, believing that pain is the only path to progress. We wear tiredness like a trophy and uphold "discipline" as a virtue, even when it's simply punishing ourselves. (See Chapter 5 for rest science; here we put the ideas to work.)

I once had a friend who, by all accounts, was a model of fitness. She was a marathon runner, a dedicated yogi, and a strict vegetarian. From the outside, her life looked incredibly healthy. But in conversations, I learned the truth. Her running was a form of self-punishment for a meal she felt was "unclean." Her yoga was an obligation, a way to maintain an image of peace, not a source of it. And her diet was a source of constant anxiety, a daily battle with herself. She was not in a relationship with her body; she was in a war. The hustle had taught her that her body was an enemy to be conquered, a project to be perfected, and she was miserable in the process.

The soft rebel knows this to be a lie.

Science Note: Psychologists use the term *orthorexia* to describe an unhealthy obsession with "clean eating." While the goal begins as health, it often leads to food anxiety, social isolation, and guilt after eating "imperfect" foods. In other words: the pursuit of purity can become its own form of sickness (Bratman, 1997; Dunn & Bratman, 2016).

Soft Rebel Move: Swap one "should-do" workout for a "want-to" movement this week.

Permission Slip: You don't have to earn your food. You don't have to burn off your joy.

Cozy Victory: Eating dessert without apology—and savoring every bite.

A Gentle and Respectful Relationship

The soft rebellion in wellness is a return to a more gentle, intuitive, and respectful relationship with our bodies. It is an act of letting go of the ideals of perfection and embracing the wisdom that our bodies have always held. This is not a rebellion against health; it is a rebellion against the toxic culture that has turned health into a competition.

The core of this revolution is to shift your mindset from one of control and punishment to one of trust and respect. Your body is not a project to be fixed; it is a partner to be listened to. The rebellion is in learning to tune out the noise of social media and diet culture and tune into the quiet, powerful wisdom of your own intuition.

1. Joyful Movement Over Punishing Exercise

The hustle tells us that a good workout has to be grueling, painful, and exhausting. The soft rebel knows that movement should be a source of joy and energy, not a form of punishment for what we ate.

This could be a long walk in nature, a dance class, a session of gentle stretching, or a bike ride. The goal is to find movement that makes you feel alive, not drained.

Science Note: Research on exercise adherence shows that people are far more likely to stick with movement they enjoy. Joyful activity builds consistency and long-term health; punishing workouts often lead to burnout and abandonment (Deci & Ryan, 2008; Teixeira et al., 2012).

Otis and Me

For me, joyful movement often looks like walking with Otis. I've had him for ten years now. He's truly the best dog—

calm, loyal, and endlessly patient (unless we're at the vet, where his anxiety can rival my worst panic attacks). As a goldendoodle, he's always had plenty of energy, so daily walks became a ritual early on.

Over the years, those walks turned into something more than exercise. They've become a form of meditation. I slip on my shoes, pop in an audiobook, and we take the long route. It's our way of greeting the day—his paws on the pavement, my mind slowly unclenching. On days when we skip, both of us feel it. He looks restless, and I feel off-kilter.

Now that Otis is older, I'm careful about the length. His joints don't carry him quite as far as they used to. But even shortened, our walks remain one of my greatest joys—a way to care for him, care for myself, and honor the partnership between us. Movement, I've learned, doesn't have to look like miles logged or calories burned. Sometimes it looks like ten thousand steps, and sometimes it looks like a slow stroll with a dog you love.

- **Cozy Victory:** A walk with your dog that feeds your soul as much as your body.

My Half-Marathon Lesson

For years, I thought running was the ultimate proof of discipline. Training for a half-marathon felt like a rite of passage—a way to prove I could push myself to the limit. But the reality was injury stacked on injury. I spent months in rehab, limping through physical therapy, nursing one tendon while straining another.

Eventually, I had to face the truth: my body couldn't handle long-distance running. At first, I felt ashamed. Was I giving up? Was I weak? But over time, I realized the rebellion wasn't in pushing harder—it was in listening. My body wasn't betraying me; it was protecting me. Choosing to stop long-distance training wasn't a failure; it was a matter of respect.

2. Nourishment Over Restriction

For too long, diet culture has convinced us to label food as "good" or "bad," turning nourishment into a battlefield. We are conditioned to think about food in terms of calories, macros, and "good" versus "bad" foods. The rebellion is in letting go of this all-or-nothing mindset and returning to a relationship with food that is intuitive and nourishing.

🧠 **Science Note:** Studies on mindful eating show that people who slow down and pay attention to food experience better digestion and less stress—even if their overall diet "quality" doesn't change. Awareness matters as much as ingredients (Kristeller & Wolever, 2011; Mason et al., 2016; Harvard Health Publishing, 2021).

Soft Rebel Move: Try one meal this week without multitasking—no scrolling, no email, just you and your food.

3. The mind-body Connection

The hustle separates the mind and the body. It treats our physical health and our mental health as two separate things, but the soft rebel knows that they are inextricably linked.

Practical Steps for a Mindful Body

This rebellion is not about a new routine; it's about a new mindset. Here are some simple, practical steps to begin your journey toward a more gentle and respectful relationship with your body.

- **Conduct a Joyful Movement Audit.** Make a list of every physical activity you have ever genuinely enjoyed—gardening, dancing, walking with a pet, stretching before bed. Prioritize these over punishing routines.

- **Practice Mindful Eating.** Sit with your meal. Notice flavors, textures, hunger, and fullness cues. Presence transforms food from fuel alone into nourishment.

- **Try a Body Compassion Practice.** Thank your body for one thing daily—its lungs that breathe, legs that carry, or arms that hug. Gratitude softens criticism.

- **Reclaim Rest.** Sleep is not indulgence—it's biology. The hustle says earn it; the soft rebel knows you're designed for it.

- **Ritualize Recovery.** Create rituals that restore—stretching before bed, Sunday naps, or warm baths. Build repair into your week.

- **Practice Body Neutrality.** You don't have to love every inch of your body. Start with respect: *I value what my body does, even if I don't love how it looks.*

🧠 **Science Note:** Sleep deprivation impairs decision-making, slows immune response, and raises the risk of anxiety and depression. Adequate rest is not optional—it's foundational (Killgore, 2010; Cohen et al., 2009; Baglioni et al., 2011; Palmer & Dahl, 2017).

Soft Rebel Move: Schedule bedtime as fiercely as any meeting.

Cozy Victory: Waking up rested instead of wired.

Rebel Reflection:

- When have I treated my body like an enemy instead of an ally?
- What movement feels like play to me?
- How do I want to *feel* in my body—not just look?
- Where does rest currently fit (or not fit) in my routine?
- What food or ritual makes me feel most cared for?
- How might I show respect to my body this week—without tying it to performance?

Closing: The Body as Home

The soft rebel's relationship with their body is one of respect, intuition, and peace. By letting go of the pursuit of perfection and embracing a more gentle and kind approach to health and wellness, you are laying groundwork of strength that will serve you for the rest of your life. In a world that tells us to conquer our bodies, the greatest rebellion is to choose to love and care for them instead.

Chapter 13: Creating Your Sanctuary

✦ ✦ ✦

A sanctuary isn't a place you find.
It's something you build,
choice by choice, breath by breath,
until your life starts to feel like home again.

We have spent the last chapters on an inward journey—redefining success, embracing rest, and cultivating authenticity within ourselves. But for this revolution to be sustainable, it must have a physical home. Your quiet revolution needs a sanctuary, a physical and mental space that supports your newfound values and protects you from the noise of the world.

In a culture that tells us to be "on" all the time, our homes have become extensions of our offices. Our minds are filled with endless to-do lists, worries, and digital notifications. Our schedules are packed with back-to-back meetings and social obligations. We are surrounded by physical possessions we don't need, digital information we can't process, and commitments that leave us exhausted. This is the clutter of the hustle, and it is a direct path to anxiety.

Our minds are not built to be "on" all the time, yet the modern world demands it. Every unread email, every social notification, and every overflowing closet acts like a low-grade stressor, subtly chipping away at our sense of calm. This constant barrage of digital and physical clutter prevents our nervous system from ever fully settling down. We carry the weight of an endless to-do list in our minds and a visual symphony of chaos in our homes, leaving no space for rest, reflection, or peace. The modern sanctuary is not about achieving an empty, minimalist aesthetic; it is about creating a space where our minds and bodies can finally exhale.

The soft rebel knows that a chaotic outer world will create a chaotic inner world. A cluttered home leads to a cluttered mind. An overstuffed calendar leads to a constant feeling of being overwhelmed. The soft rebellion, therefore, requires a conscious effort to declutter your home, your schedule, and your mind.

The hustle has convinced us that a cluttered life is a sign of productivity, a badge of honor. We look at a full calendar and think, "I must be important." We look at a house full of possessions and think, "I must be successful." But this is a lie. This clutter is a steady, low drumbeat of stress that drains our energy and makes it hard to find a moment of genuine peace. A home full of unused items is a home of unresolved decisions. A mind full of digital noise is a mind that cannot be present. A schedule with no white space is a life with no room for joy.

I once knew a woman who lived in a beautiful, sprawling home that was overflowing with stuff. She had closets full of clothes she never wore, a garage full of boxes she hadn't opened in years, and a schedule that was so packed she barely had time to sleep. She was, by all accounts, very busy. But when she spoke, she was taut with anxiety. Her physical and mental clutter had become a prison. She had built a beautiful life, but she had no space in it to simply breathe.

The soft rebel knows that freedom is not about having more; it's about having what you truly need and letting go of the rest.

Science Note: Visual clutter increases "attentional load," nudging your brain into a mild threat posture (hello, cortisol). Conversely, tidy, low-stimulus spaces lower arousal and help your nervous system idle in "rest-and-digest" (Saxbe & Repetti, 2010; McMains & Kastner, 2011; Kaplan, 1995).

Soft Rebel Move: Pick one view you see daily (nightstand, kitchen counter). Clear it completely tonight. Notice your body tomorrow morning.

☑ **Permission Slip:** Empty space isn't wasted—it's restorative.

• **Cozy Victory:** A single uncluttered surface that makes your shoulders drop.

The Power of Sanctuary

The soft rebellion is about creating a sanctuary, not as a luxury, but as a necessity. A sanctuary is a place where you feel safe, a place where you can be your true, authentic, and imperfect self without judgment. It is a space—physical, digital, and temporal—designed to support you, not overwhelm you.

The Physical Sanctuary

Your home should be a refuge from the world. When your physical space is calm and intentional, your mind follows. This isn't about white walls and two throw pillows. It's about **fit**: fewer, loved items; simple zones for how you actually live; light, scent, and sound that help your body downshift. (See Chapter 2 for the stress biology; this section focuses on practical switches back to parasympathetic repair.)

- **Zones over rooms.** A reading corner can live in a studio; a "phone-free nook" can be a single chair by a window.

- **Soothing inputs.** Soft lighting in the evening, natural light in the morning, warm textures, and a touch of nature (plants, wood, stone) evoke a sense of safety.

- **A landing strip.** A small tray + hooks by the door prevents the "keys-wallet-mail" explosion that starts the night with stress.

🧠 **Science Note:** Natural elements (plants, daylight, nature sounds) are linked to lower blood pressure and stress. Even a small plant or opening blinds in the morning can shift mood and focus (Ulrich, 1984; Bringslimark, Hartig, & Patil, 2009; Alvarsson, Wiens, & Nilsson, 2010).

The Digital Sanctuary

In our modern world, our minds are constantly bombarded by digital noise. Creating a sanctuary requires fierce protection of your attention.

- **Notifications as gatekeepers.** Turn off badges for anything that isn't a true alert.
- **One-screen home.** Keep only 6—9 essentials on your home screen; move everything else to a second page or App Library.
- **Device bedtime.** Screens off 60 minutes before sleep; a cheap alarm clock frees your phone from the nightstand.

🧠 **Science Note:** Evening blue light suppresses melatonin, delays REM onset, and fragments sleep. A darker, quieter last hour tells your brain: "We're safe. Power down" (Cajochen et al., 2005; Chang et al., 2015; Harvard Health Publishing, 2012).

The Scheduling Sanctuary

The greatest act of rebellion is leaving white space on your calendar. White space isn't laziness—it's capacity.

- **Hard holds.** Pre-block restorative time (walks, reading, naps) is like any meeting.

- **Admin islands.** Cluster low-value tasks (email, errands) so they stop colonizing every hour.

- **Buffer zones.** 10 minutes between commitments prevents the "spilled coffee" effect, where one delay ruins the whole day.

🧠 **Science Note:** Task switching carries a cognitive "switch cost." Batch work reduces error rates and preserves willpower (Monsell, 2003; Rogers & Monsell, 1995; Mark, Gudith, & Klocke, 2008).

The rebellion is not about a new routine; it is about a new way of being. See your environment—physical and digital—as an extension of your nervous system. When you create a sanctuary, you're telling your body and brain: **you're safe here.**

Practical Steps to Create Your Sanctuary

Creating a sanctuary is not a one-time event; it is a practice.

1. **Define Your Sanctuary's Purpose.**
   Before you start decluttering, ask: "What do I want this space to *do* for me?" Rest? Creativity? Connection? Purpose becomes your filter. If you want rest, reduce visual noise in the bedroom. If you

want creativity, keep tools visible and distractions hidden.

2. **The Gentle Physical Declutter.**
Start small. One drawer, one shelf, one surface. Ask: *Do I love this? Does it serve me now?* Release "aspirational clutter" (hobbies you don't enjoy, sizes that don't fit, gadgets you never use). Donate, recycle, or give items a grateful goodbye.

3. **The Digital Declutter.**
Turn off non-essential notifications. Unsubscribe ruthlessly. Create inbox rules for newsletters. Set your phone to grayscale after 9 p.m. (less dopamine, less doomscrolling).

4. **The Scheduling Declutter.**
Block "sanctuary hours" each week: a quiet walk, a long bath, a book in bed, or simply tea in silence. Treat these as non-negotiable.

5. **Sensory Tune-Up (Small Inputs, Big Calm).**
    a. Evening light: switch to warm lamps; dim overheads.
    b. Sound: one "sanctuary playlist" (lo-fi, nature sounds, or silence).
    c. Scent: lavender or cedar in the evening, citrus in the morning.
    d. Temperature: cooler bedrooms (most sleep best ~65–67°F).

6. **The Two-Minute Reset.**
Choose a hotspot (desk, sink, coffee table). Two minutes, once a day, to restore it. Small resets compound into big calm.

7. **The "One In, One Out" Rule.**
   If something new comes in, something goes out. Keeps growth intentional.

8. **Create a Phone-Free Island.**
   One surface (nightstand, dining table) becomes sacred territory. No devices allowed. Protect a sliver of analog life.

Soft Rebel Move: Put a weekly "Home Hour" on your calendar: 20 minutes to reset a hotspot, 20 to prep meals/snacks, 20 to set up your favorite corner.

Permission Slip: You don't need a perfect home. You need a gentle one.

Cozy Victory: Lighting one candle and reading two pages in your reclaimed chair.

Clothing Declutter Ritual

I live in a tiny house built in the 1920s, which means closet space is scarce. At first, that felt like a limitation, but over time it has become a quiet blessing. The small space forces me to stay intentional. Every two or three months, I do a full sweep of my clothes—drawers, closet, and all. I pull everything out, try things on, and sort them into piles: donate, sell, or keep.

I also have a fourth category I call "hold." These are items I'm not sure about—things I've regretted parting with too quickly in the past. Instead of making a rash decision, I tuck them into a separate box and revisit them six months later. By then, a new season has rolled in, and I can see clearly whether I really missed them or not.

This ritual keeps my small storage spaces clean and manageable, but it also keeps me accountable. It's a way of checking in with myself: Am I buying more than I need? Am I holding onto things out of habit rather than out of joy? It's not just about closets—it's about creating a sanctuary where even the smallest spaces feel intentional and thoughtfully designed.

Room-by-Room Micro-Sanctuaries (Build where it matters most)

- **Entryway:** Hooks + tray + basket = your landing strip. Lower chaos on arrival lowers evening stress.

- **Kitchen:** Clear one counter. Put a bowl of fruit and your favorite mug there. Make water and tea the easy choice.

- **Bedroom:** Blackout curtains, cool temp, no laptop. A book on the nightstand, not a browser.

- **Workspace:** Single-task desk. Everything else lives in a basket you put away at day's end.

- **Bathroom:** "Spa shelf": one lotion, one scent, one soft towel. Ritual beats renovation.

- **Outdoor:** A chair by a window, a tiny balcony plant, a sun-patch on the floor—your micro dose of nature.

🧠 **Science Note:** Even brief nature exposure (a window view, houseplants, a 10-minute walk) lowers rumination and improves mood. "Green time" is nervous-system nutrition (Ulrich, 1984; Kaplan, 1995; Bratman et al., 2015).

Boundaries That Keep Your Sanctuary Safe

- **Visitor policy:** You don't owe anyone a drop-in. Schedule hosts *you* have energy for.

- **Work cutoff:** A phrase you can say (and an auto-reply you can set): "I'm offline after 6. I'll reply in the morning."

- **Media diet:** Choose what comes in (news windows, not news drip). Curate feeds like you curate furniture. (As introduced in Chapter 1, comparison is built-in—and Chapter 3 shows how the feed weaponizes it. Here we'll stay with the practice.)

Soft Rebel Move: Put your values where your router is—set a nightly Wi-Fi auto-off for non-work devices.

Cozy Victory: Your living room at 9 p.m.: lamplight, a blanket, and the sound of pages turning.

If You Share Your Space

Sanctuary isn't about control; it's about collaboration.

- **Co-create a "calm contract."** Three things everyone can agree to (shoes at the door, no phones at the table, bedtime lighting).

- **Personal zones.** Each person gets one small area to style and protect.

- **Sanctuary signals.** Noise-canceling headphones, a closed door, or a candle lit = "please limit interruptions."

☑ **Permission Slip:** Your need for quiet is valid—even in a full house.

Rebel Reflection: Designing a Home That Holds You

- What do I want my sanctuary to *do* for me this season (rest, create, connect, heal)?
- Which single view in my home stresses me out the most—and what 10-minute action would help?
- Where can I carve a phone-free island this week?
- What hour can I protect as white space on my calendar?
- Which small ritual (light, sound, scent, texture) tells my nervous system "you're safe"?

Closing

The hustle says: fill every room, every minute, every screen. Your soft rebellion says: **make room.** A sanctuary is not perfection—it's permission. It's the chair by the window, the quiet corner of your calendar, the nightstand with a single book. It's the brave, ordinary choice to build a life that lets your body and mind finally exhale.

Chapter 14: Your Personal Manifesto

✦ ✦ ✦

You don't need a revolution to begin again.
Just a promise to live by your own quiet truths —
and to keep choosing them,
even when the world forgets how.

You have now done the difficult and beautiful work of introspection. You've looked at the hustle's most powerful lies and found the courage to reject them. You have redefined success on your own terms, embraced rest, discovered your authentic voice, and taken back control of your career, your finances, and your well-being.

But this is not a path you walk once and for all. The world will not stop trying to pull you back into its rhythm.

This chapter is about a final, crucial act of soft rebellion: creating your **personal manifesto**.

A manifesto is not a political document or a set of rigid rules. It is a clear, written statement of your values and your personal definition of success. It is your ultimate guide, a map for the road ahead, and an anchor to hold you steady when the winds of the hustle try to pull you off course.

In a world filled with noise, a manifesto is a source of profound clarity. The hustle thrives on confusion. It wants you to be constantly running, too busy to stop and ask yourself what you truly want. It offers a million shiny objects and a thousand different definitions of success, hoping you'll grab onto one and start running without ever questioning if it's the right direction for you.

Your manifesto is the antidote. It is a bold, simple statement that says:

"I know what I want. I know who I am. And I am no longer available for what doesn't serve me."

The manifesto is the final act of solidifying your rebellion—turning abstract ideas and personal breakthroughs into a tangible, living document. It is the bridge between your internal world and your external actions. The process of writing it down makes your values real and revisit-able.

Think of it as your own **anchor in a storm**. When a new career opportunity arises that promises more money but less time, your manifesto can remind you that your personal definition of success is based on freedom, not income. When a social media post makes you feel like you are falling behind, your manifesto can remind you that your worth is not tied to likes or accomplishments. (See Chapter 5 for rest science; here we put the ideas to work.)

🧠 **Science Note:** Psychologists call this the *encoding effect*. When you write something by hand, you engage more brain regions linked to memory, reflection, and problem-solving. Your manifesto isn't just a list—it's a neurological reinforcement of your deepest values (Craik & Tulving, 1975; Karpicke & Roediger, 2008; Mueller & Oppenheimer, 2014).

✺ **Soft Rebel Move:** Jot down one value or principle on a sticky note. Put it on your bathroom mirror. Every morning, it's the first voice you hear—your own.

☑ **Permission Slip:** Your manifesto is valid even if it lives in a notebook no one else ever sees.

● **Cozy Victory:** The moment you reread your manifesto before a tough meeting and feel your shoulders unclench.

A Step-by-Step Guide to Writing Your Manifesto

Writing your manifesto isn't about perfection. It's about honesty. You can jot it in a journal, type it on your laptop, or scrawl it on the back of a napkin. What matters is that you do it.

Step 1: The Core Beliefs Audit

Reflect on the foundational questions of your soft rebellion:

- What is my personal definition of success?
- What is "enough" for me?
- What are my non-negotiable values?
- What brings me genuine joy and peace?

These are the building blocks of your manifesto. Take your time—your answers will form the foundation of everything else.

Soft Rebel Move: Answer one question each night for a week instead of trying to tackle them all at once. Small reflections add up.

Cozy Victory: Reading back over your answers and realizing they already sound like the beginnings of a manifesto.

Step 2: Define Your Rebellion

A manifesto requires not only clarity about what you stand for, but also what you're refusing to accept. Hustle culture thrives in vagueness. Naming your rebellion shines light in the corners where it hides.

Ask yourself:

- What aspects of the hustle am I actively rejecting? The pressure to always be "on"? The belief that busy equals worthy?

- What toxic behaviors or mindsets am I no longer available for? Constant comparison? Perfectionism? The low-grade hum of "not enough"? (As introduced in Chapter 1, comparison is built-in—and Chapter 3 shows how the feed weaponizes it. Here we'll stay with the practice.)

Write these down plainly, almost like a "No Longer Accepting Applications" list.

☑ **Permission Slip:** You don't need to rebel against everything. One clear "no" is more powerful than ten vague ones.

● **Cozy Victory:** Flipping through your notes later and seeing "I am no longer available for self-judgment" circled three times in bold ink.

Step 3: Articulate Your Guiding Principles

Now comes the heart of your manifesto: turning your beliefs and rejections into *active, guiding principles*. Use strong, personal language.

Examples:

- Instead of *"I believe in rest,"* write: *"I will prioritize rest as a non-negotiable part of my week, and I will not feel guilty for it."*

- Instead of *"I'm tired of consumerism,"* write: *"I will spend in alignment with my values, not my impulses. I will find joy in what I already own."*

- Instead of *"I want to be authentic,"* write: *"I will show up as my genuine self, even when it feels uncomfortable."*

Five to ten principles are plenty. Think of them as handrails—you don't need dozens, just a few strong ones to steady you when the world tilts.

Soft Rebel Move: Use "I will" language—it cues your brain to future action, not passive belief.

Science Note: Studies on *implementation intentions* show that using "I will" statements increases follow-through by priming the brain's goal-setting networks (Gollwitzer, 1999; Gollwitzer & Sheeran, 2006).

Step 4: Make It a Living Document

Your manifesto isn't finished once it's written. It's alive. It should grow with you.

Revisit it every few months: reread, reflect, and revise. Cross out what no longer fits. Add new guiding principles as your life shifts. Your manifesto is not about proving consistency—it's about staying aligned with who you are becoming.

Permission Slip: Editing your manifesto isn't a sign you got it wrong—it's proof you're paying attention.

Cozy Victory: The day you open your manifesto six months later and realize it already predicted the choice you're making now.

🧠 **Science Note:** Decision fatigue is real. We only have so much willpower each day. A clear manifesto reduces mental load—no need to agonize over every request, offer, or trend. You already know what fits (Baumeister et al., 1998; Vohs et al., 2008).

Living Your Manifesto

Writing it down is powerful. But living it—that's where your quiet rebellion becomes unstoppable.

Your Manifesto as a Decision-Making Tool

Every tough decision is a chance to return home to your manifesto. Ask: *"Does this align with my manifesto?"* If the answer is no, you've got a clear and guilt-free reason to decline.

Your Manifesto as a Shield

The world will try to drag you back into the chaos. Your manifesto allows you to set boundaries without overexplaining. A simple "I'm focusing on a slower pace right now" is enough.

The Power of the Spoken Word

Saying your manifesto out loud deepens your commitment. Share it with someone you trust. Speaking your truth activates accountability and invites meaningful support.

🌱 **Soft Rebel Move:** Read your manifesto to yourself once a week. Out loud. Let your own voice be your anchor.

🧠 **Science Note:** Neuroscience shows that goal clarity boosts dopamine—the brain's motivation signal. Unlike hustle-driven dopamine (fleeting "likes," purchases, promotions), manifesto-driven clarity produces steadier, longer-lasting motivation (Schultz, 2007; Berridge & Robinson, 2003; Aarts & Dijksterhuis, 2000).

The Final Act of Self-Sovereignty

Your personal manifesto is more than words. It's a declaration that you belong to yourself.

It says:

- I am no longer available for what drains me.
- I am free to define success on my own terms.
- I am building a life that is intentionally, beautifully my own.

In a world that tries to define you at every turn, the reward for living your manifesto is profound: **peace, purpose, and genuine freedom.**

☑ **Permission Slip:** Your manifesto doesn't have to be "finished." It just has to be yours.

● **Cozy Victory:** A page filled with your own handwriting—proof that you've chosen yourself.

Chapter 15: The Quiet Revolution Continues

The world may never notice your quiet revolution.
But you will —
in the peace that follows every gentle no,
every small act of coming home to yourself.

You have learned to redefine success, reclaim your rest, live with authenticity, and build a sanctuary for your mind and body. You have a personal manifesto—a clear statement of your values that keeps you grounded. But the most important lesson of the soft rebellion is this: the journey is not a one-time event; it is a daily, evolving practice.

The work you have done to this point is the foundation. The true revolution lies in the quiet, consistent act of living these principles every single day, for the rest of your life.

The world will not stop. The hustle will not disappear. New pressures will arise, new comparisons will present themselves, and new anxieties will try to take root. This is why the soft rebellion is not a temporary solution but a long-term strategy for a life of sustained freedom, peace, and joy. (As introduced in Chapter 1 and Chapter 3).

The Compound Effect of a Quiet Life

The principles you've embraced may feel small in a world that celebrates grand gestures. However, over time, these small acts have a profound cumulative effect.

A single day of choosing rest instead of hustle may not feel revolutionary. But a year of choosing rest will fundamentally change your relationship with yourself. One decision to say "no" may feel like a small rebellion. But a decade of honoring your manifesto will build a life that is deeply, beautifully your own.

Over time, these choices create a foundation so solid it cannot be shaken by the whims of the outside world.

- **You cultivate True Freedom.** The hustle tells you that freedom is having enough money to buy anything you want. The soft rebel knows that true freedom is the mental and emotional space to choose your life based on your values, not outside pressure. This comes from financial peace, firm boundaries, and the clarity to say no without guilt.

- **You find Lasting Joy.** The hustle's happiness is fleeting—a promotion, a purchase, a compliment. The soft rebel's joy is steady, an internal state that comes from living aligned with your authentic self.

- **You build Invaluable Resilience.** Hustle life leaves you fragile, where every setback feels catastrophic. A life built on rest, purpose, and connection is durable. The inevitable storms of life will still come—but they will not shatter you. You have an anchor: your values, your manifesto, your village.

Science Note: Psychologists call this *habit stacking*. Small, repeated choices rewire your brain's default pathways, making calm and clarity the "automatic" response instead of stress. Over months and years, your nervous system starts to expect peace (Clear, 2018; Lally et al., 2010; Graybiel, 2008).

Soft Rebel Move: Pick one anchor ritual (morning walk, journaling, weekly phone-free evening). Stick with it for a season. Let it become part of your foundation.

Cozy Victory: Looking back a year from now and realizing the tiny habit you barely noticed has reshaped your whole rhythm.

☑ **Permission Slip:** Freedom doesn't mean having it all—it means having space to choose.

The Journey Continues

The quiet revolution is not a finish line to cross and then forget. It is an ongoing practice, a constant choice. The world will always be there, tempting you back into its rhythm. Your manifesto is your compass, but you still have to choose to follow it.

And as you grow, your rebellion will grow with you. The boundaries you needed in your twenties will not be the same as the ones you'll need in your forties. Your definition of success may shift. What once felt like rebellion might one day feel like second nature. Your manifesto is a living document—a reflection of your evolving self.

The journey is not about never getting lost. It's about always knowing how to find your way back home to your values.

Consider Pete. In his twenties, his rebellion was saying no to an overbearing job. In his thirties, with a young family, it became about protecting family time and finding financial peace. In his forties, it shifted again—slowing down, prioritizing creativity, and mentoring others. His path hasn't been linear. There were setbacks, doubts, and seasons that felt like failure. But through it all, he returned to his manifesto, his values, and his commitment to peace. His life isn't "perfect," but it is purposeful. And that quiet joy would never have been found on the hustle's path.

💬 **Science Note:** Longitudinal studies show that *values clarity* is one of the strongest predictors of resilience. People who understand what matters most tend to bounce back faster from crises, setbacks, and transitions (Seligman & Csikszentmihalyi, 2000; Van Breda, 2001; Kashdan et al., 2006).

- **Cozy Victory:** Realizing your path doesn't need to be straight to be meaningful. Curves, pauses, and even detours can still carry you home.

The Ripple Effect Amplified

Your personal rebellion is powerful. But its reach extends far beyond you.

You are a living testament to a different way of being. By quietly choosing rest, presence, and authenticity, you model a new definition of success.

- You show others it's possible to be ambitious without being stressed.
- You prove success doesn't require burnout.
- You demonstrate that happiness doesn't come from a chase but from a pace.

Your children, your nieces and nephews, your community—when they see you living differently, they're given permission to choose differently too.

The greatest contribution you can make to the world is not to become the perfect hero of hustle. It is to become a peaceful, grounded, whole human being. Your calm presence is a gift. Your genuine joy becomes a beacon. Your quiet rebellion is not selfish—it is the most generous act of all. You fill your own cup so that you can overflow into the lives of others.

- **Soft Rebel Move:** Share one of your rebellion choices with someone younger—a child, a mentee, a friend just starting out. You may be planting a seed you'll never see bloom.

- **Cozy Victory:** Hearing someone say, "I watched you slow down—and it gave me permission to do the same."

Rebel Reflection: Continuing Your Rebellion

- Which small act of rebellion do I want to repeat daily?

- How has my definition of freedom, joy, or resilience shifted this year?

- Who in my life might benefit from seeing me live this way?

The journey continues, and so does the quiet revolution. Keep going. Keep choosing the gentle path. Keep honoring your true self. The world is waiting for you.

Chapter 16: A New Beginning

✦ ✦ ✦

Every soft rebellion begins again.
Not with noise or grand declarations,
but with one quiet choice to live differently —
starting now.

You have now reached the final chapter of this book. But this is not an ending. This is a beginning. The journey of soft rebellion is not a destination you arrive at after reading a final page. It is a path you step onto, one intentional choice at a time.

The knowledge you have gained is powerful, but its true power lies not in understanding, but in action.

The soft rebellion is not a theory; it is a lived experience. It is a revolution that begins not in the streets, but in the quietest corners of your own life. It is the courage to begin, even when the world tells you to wait. It is the bravery to take a single, small step, even when the path ahead is uncertain. This final chapter is a call to action. It is an invitation to move from contemplation to commitment, and to begin your new life today.

The Call to Courage

The first step is always the hardest. The fear of the unknown is powerful, and the voice of the hustle is persistent. It will tell you that you are not ready, that you need to be more prepared, that you should wait for the "perfect" moment.

But the soft rebel knows: a quiet revolution does not wait for perfect conditions. It begins right where you are, with what you have.

The courage of the soft rebel is not about one grand, heroic act. It is about a thousand small, daily acts of defiance. It is the courage to leave one email unread. The courage to say "no" to a social obligation you don't want to attend. The courage to take a ten-minute walk in silence without your phone.

These small acts may not seem like much, but they are the bedrock of a life of peace. They are the daily decisions that, over time, build a profound sense of freedom.

✅ **Permission Slip:** You don't need a five-year plan to start your quiet revolution. You only need today.

• **Cozy Victory:** Saying no to one thing tonight—and realizing the world keeps spinning.

💭 **Science Note:** Behavioral science shows that "micro-actions" (tiny, consistent behaviors) are the strongest predictors of long-term change. Change sticks when it starts small (Lally et al., 2010; Amabile & Kramer, 2011; Fogg, 2019).

Do not be afraid of "failure." The soft rebellion has no failure, only learning. When you fall back into old habits, it is not weakness—it is proof you are human. Every stumble is a new opportunity to practice grace and begin again.

The courage is in the getting up, not in the never falling.

The Legacy of a Gentle Life

Your choice to live this way is not just for you. Your peaceful life is your greatest gift to the world.

The hustle is built on the myth of more. The soft rebellion is built on the truth of enough. By living with intentionality and contentment, you challenge the dominant cultural narrative.

The way you spend your time, the people you love, the way you treat your body—it all tells a story. A story that says:

"I am enough. My life is enough. And I am not available for what doesn't serve my peace."

Your life becomes a manifesto. It is a quiet declaration that your worth is not in what you do, but in who you are. The wealth of your life is not measured in your bank account, but in your purpose, your peace, and your relationships. This is the true measure of a life well-lived.

- **Soft Rebel Move:** Live one guiding principle out loud this week. Let your actions do the teaching.
- **Cozy Victory:** Hearing someone you love say, "I can see you're calmer—and it makes me feel calmer too."

This is your legacy: a peaceful presence, a calm soul, a life lived with integrity and joy. It will inspire others not with a shout, but with a whisper.

Your New Beginning

The journey ahead is not a sprint; it is a marathon. It will require patience, kindness, and commitment to yourself. But you are not alone. You have the tools, the knowledge, and the courage to begin.

I invite you to close your eyes and picture the life you truly want. A life of peace. A life of purpose. A life filled with genuine connection. Do not let the world tell you this life is impossible. It is waiting for you.

The time to begin is not tomorrow. It is not when you have more money, more time, or a new job. The time to begin is now. Your quiet revolution starts in this moment, in this room, with a single, intentional choice.

By choosing this path, you are not giving up your life—you are finally beginning to live it. The hustle promises you everything but gives you nothing. The soft rebellion promises you nothing but gives you everything.

The soft rebellion is not just a journey away from burnout; it is a journey toward freedom. The freedom to choose your time. The freedom to define your worth. The freedom to live authentically.

In a world of noise and distraction, your quiet presence is a radical act of resistance. You are not missing out by stepping away. You are finally showing up for the one thing that matters most: your own life.

Welcome to your new beginning. Go now, and begin your quiet revolution. The world is waiting for you.

Living the Rebellion: Your Toolkit

You have completed the journey of soft rebellion. You have learned to redefine success, to listen to your body, and to build a life of intention. The work is not over, but the tools are now in your hands.

Use this toolkit whenever you feel lost or pulled back into the hustle:

The Quick Audits

- **Values Audit:** Am I living in alignment with what matters most?

- **Rest Audit:** Am I truly resting—or just not working?

- **Authenticity Audit:** Am I showing up as my true self—or performing for others?

- **Financial Audit:** Am I spending to fill a void—or in ways that bring peace?

- **Connection Audit:** Who nourishes me, and who drains me?

- **Body Audit:** Am I treating my body with respect or punishment?

- **Sanctuary Audit:** Does my environment make me feel safe and calm?

☑ **Permission Slip:** You don't have to do everything. Choose one tool when you need it.

● **Cozy Victory:** The relief of knowing you already have what you need to start again—anytime.

Your First 7 Days: A Gentle Start

The revolution begins with one small, intentional choice. You don't have to change everything at once. Use this simple 7-day challenge to build momentum and begin your new life. Each day focuses on a different principle from the book and is designed to take less than 15 minutes.

- **Day 1:** The Digital Detox. Give your nervous system a break—turn off the pings, dings, and pop-ups that aren't essential. Make a conscious choice to check your devices on your terms, not theirs.

- **Day 2:** The Guilt-Free Break. Take a 15-minute break in the middle of your day to do absolutely nothing. Close your eyes, stretch, or just stare out a window. Do not feel guilty.

- **Day 3:** The Mindful Meal. Sit down for one meal and eat without any distractions (no phone, no TV). Pay attention to the flavors, the textures, and the experience of eating.

- **Day 4:** The Kindness to Your Body. Stand in front of a mirror and find one thing you can thank your body for. Your hands, your feet, your eyes—whatever it is, say thank you.

- **Day 5:** The Single "No." Say "no" to one thing you don't genuinely want to do. It can be an invitation, a request, or a new obligation. Practice the power of the word "no."

- **Day 6:** The Declutter. Choose one small area to declutter. It could be a junk drawer, a single shelf, or your purse. Get rid of anything that doesn't serve you.

- **Day 7:** The Gentle Walk. Take a 20-minute walk outside. Leave your phone at home or in your pocket and simply pay attention to the world around you.

Welcome to your new beginning.

Epilogue: Still Becoming

◆ ◆ ◆

The quiet revolution never really ends...

As we close this book, I want to remind you of something important: I am still right here in the messy middle with you. Writing these pages didn't mean I had all the answers—it meant I was brave enough to gather what I've learned so far and share it, even while I'm still learning, stumbling, and growing.

Being a soft rebel isn't about perfection; it's about presence. It's choosing authenticity when it would be easier to perform, choosing rest when the world shouts for more, and choosing to live by your own values—even when that choice feels small or unseen.

If anything here resonated with you, let it be this: you don't have to have it all figured out to start living differently. Progress isn't about crossing some finish line; it's about showing up each day with gentleness, intention, and courage.

I'm walking this road too. Some days I'll get it right. Other days I'll trip, falter, and have to begin again. And that's okay—because the untamed life isn't about getting it perfect. It's about living it real.

So take what serves you, leave what doesn't, and keep rewriting the story in your own way. We're all works in progress, and that's what makes the journey worth it.

Manifesto Jumpstart

Your manifesto is your compass. It is a living document that keeps you grounded and true to your values. Use this template to create your own, and revisit it often.

My Guiding Principles

- What is my personal definition of success? I believe success is...

- What is "enough" for me? My life is complete and full when...

- What values are non-negotiable in my life? I will prioritize...

- What aspects of the hustle am I actively rebelling against? I am no longer available for...

- What brings me genuine joy and peace? I will make time for...

My Commitments Based on my guiding principles, I commit to the following:

- I will prioritize rest as a non-negotiable part of my life, without guilt.

- I will spend my money in alignment with my values, not my impulse wants.

- I will show up as my genuine self, even when it is uncomfortable.

- I will protect my time from people and obligations that drain my energy.

- I will find joy in what I already have instead of constantly chasing more.

The Soft Rebellion Self Check

When you feel overwhelmed, lost, or just a little off, use these questions as a quick check-in. They are designed to bring you back to your core values and realign you with the path of peace.

- The Values Audit: Am I living a life that reflects my deepest values? Am I spending my time and energy on what truly matters to me?

- The Rest Audit: Am I truly resting, or am I just not working? Is my downtime serving to restore my body and mind, or am I simply filling it with another kind of hustle?

- The Authenticity Audit: Am I showing up as my genuine self, or am I performing for others? Is my life a reflection of my truth, or is it a curated performance for the world?

- The Financial Audit: Am I spending money to fill a void, or am I spending it on things that bring me true value and joy? Do I feel in control of my finances?

- The Connection Audit: Who in my life energizes me, and who drains me? Am I nurturing my village or am I building a shallow network?

- The Mindful Body Audit: Am I listening to my body's needs for rest, movement, and nourishment? Am I treating my body with respect and kindness, or with judgment and punishment?

- The Sanctuary Audit: Is my physical and mental space a source of calm or a source of stress? Am I making room for peace in my home, my schedule, and my mind?

✺ Want More Gentle Tools for Your Journey?

The pages you've just completed are a starting point—a way to anchor your manifesto and check in with yourself when life feels noisy. If you'd like to go deeper, I've created a set of free companion resources you can download anytime:

- **Manifesto Checklist** — a quick-reference guide to keep your values front and center.

- **Manifesto Worksheet** — a fill-in-the-blank template to help you write your guiding principles with clarity.

- **Expanded Gentle Starts** — 30 simple, doable micro-acts of soft rebellion to help you begin again, anytime.

You can grab all of these as a free bundle at https://www.fickleflashes.com/books Think of them as your pocket-sized toolkit for living the soft rebellion day by day.

● Cozy Victory: Knowing you have a gentle plan in your back pocket whenever you need to reset.

Notes and Sources:

Each reference listed here inspired or informed ideas throughout Soft Rebel, Untamed Life. Some are academic studies; others are essays, articles, and books that have shaped the collective conversation around rest, authenticity, and enoughness.

Aarts, Henk, and Ap Dijksterhuis. "Habits as Knowledge Structures: Automaticity in Goal-Directed Behavior." *Journal of Personality and Social Psychology* 78, no. 1 (2000): 53–63. https://doi.org/10.1037/0022-3514.78.1.53

Adriaanse, Marieke A., Johan C. de Ridder, and Catharine Evers. "Efficacy of Implementation Intentions on Healthy Eating: A Meta-Analysis." *Appetite* 56, no. 1 (2011): 183–193. https://doi.org/10.1016/j.appet.2010.10.012

Albertson, Elizabeth R., Kristin D. Neff, and Karen E. Dill-Shackleford. "Self-Compassion and Body Dissatisfaction in Women: A Randomized Controlled Trial of a Brief Meditation Intervention." *Mindfulness* 6, no. 3 (2015): 444–454. https://doi.org/10.1007/s12671-014-0277-3

Alvarsson, Jesper J., Stefan Wiens, and Mats E. Nilsson. "Stress Recovery During Exposure to Nature Sound and Environmental Noise." *International Journal of Environmental Research and Public Health* 7, no. 3 (2010): 1036–1046. https://doi.org/10.3390/ijerph7031036

Amabile, Teresa M., and Steven J. Kramer. *The Progress Principle: Using Small Wins to Ignite Joy, Engagement, and Creativity at Work.* Boston: Harvard Business Review Press, 2011.

American Psychological Association. "Give Me a Break." *Monitor on Psychology* 51, no. 4 (2020). https://www.apa.org/monitor/2020/04/cover-take-break

American Psychological Association. *Stress in America 2022: Concerned for the Future, Beset by Inflation.* Washington, D.C.: APA, 2022. https://www.apa.org/news/press/releases/stress

Baglioni, Chiara, Giovanni Battagliese, Barbara Feige, Kai Spiegelhalder, Dieter Nissen, Christoph Hennig, Ulrich Riemann. "Insomnia as a Predictor of Depression: A Meta-Analytic Evaluation of Longitudinal Epidemiological Studies." *Journal of Affective Disorders* 135, no. 1–3 (2011): 10–19. https://doi.org/10.1016/j.jad.2011.01.011

Baumeister, Roy F., Ellen Bratslavsky, Mark Muraven, and Dianne M. Tice. "Ego Depletion: Is the Active Self a Limited Resource?" *Journal of Personality and Social Psychology* 74, no. 5 (1998): 1252–1265. https://doi.org/10.1037/0022-3514.74.5.1252

Baumeister, Roy F., and John Tierney. *Willpower: Rediscovering the Greatest Human Strength.* New York: Penguin Press, 2011.

Ben-Shahar, Tal. *Happier: Learn the Secrets to Daily Joy and Lasting Fulfillment.* New York: McGraw-Hill, 2007.

Berridge, Kent C., and Terry E. Robinson. "Parsing Reward." *Trends in Neurosciences* 26, no. 9 (2003): 507–513. https://doi.org/10.1016/S0166-2236(03)00233-9

Bratman, Gregory N., J. Paul Hamilton, and Gretchen C. Daily. "The Impacts of Nature Experience on Human Cognitive Function and Mental Health." *Annals of*

the New York Academy of Sciences 1249, no. 1 (2012): 118–136. https://doi.org/10.1111/j.1749-6632.2011.06400.x

Bratman, Gregory N., James P. Hamilton, Kevin S. Hahn, Gregory C. Daily, and Gretchen C. Gross. "Nature Experience Reduces Rumination and Subgenual Prefrontal Cortex Activation." *Proceedings of the National Academy of Sciences* 112, no. 28 (2015): 8567–8572. https://doi.org/10.1073/pnas.1510459112

Bratman, Steven. "Health Food Junkie." *Yoga Journal*, October 1997.

Bringslimark, Tina, Terry Hartig, and Grete G. Patil. "The Psychological Benefits of Indoor Plants: A Critical Review of the Experimental Literature." *Journal of Environmental Psychology* 29, no. 4 (2009): 422–433. https://doi.org/10.1016/j.jenvp.2009.05.001

Brynjolfsson, Erik. "The Productivity Paradox of Information Technology: Review and Assessment." *Communications of the ACM* 36, no. 12 (1993): 66–77. https://doi.org/10.1145/163298.163309

Cacioppo, John T., and Louise C. Hawkley. "Perceived Social Isolation and Health: Loneliness Matters." *Social and Personality Psychology Compass* 1, no. 1 (2007): 41–54. https://doi.org/10.1111/j.1751-9004.2007.00002.x

Cajochen, Christian, Mirjam Münch, Sarah Kobialka, Kurt Kräuchi, Rolf Steiner, Peter Oelhafen, Silvia Orgül, and Anna Wirz-Justice. "High Sensitivity of Human Melatonin, Alertness, Thermoregulation, and Heart Rate to Short Wavelength Light." *Journal of Clinical Endocrinology & Metabolism* 90, no. 3 (2005): 1311–1316. https://doi.org/10.1210/jc.2004-0957

Chang, Anne-Marie, Daniel Aeschbach, Jeanne F. Duffy, and Charles A. Czeisler. "Evening Use of Light-Emitting EReaders Negatively Affects Sleep, Circadian Timing, and Next-Morning Alertness." *Proceedings of the National Academy of Sciences* 112, no. 4 (2015): 1232–1237. https://doi.org/10.1073/pnas.1418490112

Clear, James. *Atomic Habits: An Easy & Proven Way to Build Good Habits & Break Bad Ones*. New York: Avery, 2018.

Cohen, Sheldon, William J. Doyle, Cuneyt M. Alper, Denise Janicki-Deverts, and Ronald B. Turner. "Sleep Habits and Susceptibility to the Common Cold." *Archives of Internal Medicine* 169, no. 1 (2009): 62–67. https://doi.org/10.1001/archinternmed.2008.505

Craik, Fergus I. M., and Endel Tulving. "Depth of Processing and the Retention of Words in Episodic Memory." *Journal of Experimental Psychology: General* 104, no. 3 (1975): 268–294. https://doi.org/10.1037/0096-3445.104.3.268

Csikszentmihalyi, Mihaly. *Flow: The Psychology of Optimal Experience*. New York: Harper & Row, 1990.

Curran, Thomas, and Andrew P. Hill. "Perfectionism Is Increasing Over Time: A Meta-Analysis of Birth Cohort Differences From 1989 to 2016." *Psychological Bulletin* 145, no. 4 (2019): 410–429. https://doi.org/10.1037/bul0000138

DataReportal. *Digital 2023: Global Overview Report*. Kepios, January 2023. https://datareportal.com/reports/digital-2023-global-overview-report

Deci, Edward L., and Richard M. Ryan. "Self-Determination Theory: A Macrotheory of Human

Motivation, Development, and Health." *Canadian Psychology* 49, no. 3 (2008): 182–185. https://doi.org/10.1037/a0012801

Deloitte. *The Deloitte Global 2022 Gen Z and Millennial Survey.* London: Deloitte, 2022. https://www2.deloitte.com/global/en/pages/about-deloitte/articles/genzmillennialsurvey.html

Diener, Ed, Richard E. Lucas, and Christie N. Scollon. "Beyond the Hedonic Treadmill: Revising the Adaptation Theory of Well-Being." *American Psychologist* 61, no. 4 (2006): 305–314. https://doi.org/10.1037/0003-066X.61.4.305

Diener, Ed, and Martin E. P. Seligman. "Very Happy People." *Psychological Science* 13, no. 1 (2002): 81–84. https://doi.org/10.1111/1467-9280.00415

Dunn, Elizabeth W., Daniel T. Gilbert, and Timothy D. Wilson. "If Money Doesn't Make You Happy, Then You Probably Aren't Spending It Right." *Journal of Consumer Psychology* 21, no. 2 (2011): 115–125. https://doi.org/10.1016/j.jcps.2011.02.002

Dunn, Thomas M., and Steven Bratman. "On Orthorexia Nervosa: A Review of the Literature and Proposed Diagnostic Criteria." *Eating Behaviors* 21 (2016): 11–17. https://doi.org/10.1016/j.eatbeh.2015.12.006

Emmons, Robert A., and Michael E. McCullough. "Counting Blessings Versus Burdens: An Experimental Investigation of Gratitude and Subjective Well-Being in Daily Life." *Journal of Personality and Social Psychology* 84, no. 2 (2003): 377–389. https://doi.org/10.1037/0022-3514.84.2.377

Eventbrite & Harris Poll. *The FOMO Generation: How Fear of Missing Out Drives Millennial Social Media Behavior.* Eventbrite, 2014. https://eventbrite-s3.s3.amazonaws.com/marketing/Millennials_Research/Gen_PR_Final.pdf

Festinger, Leon. "A Theory of Social Comparison Processes." *Human Relations* 7, no. 2 (1954): 117–140.

Fogg, B. J. *Tiny Habits: The Small Changes That Change Everything.* Boston: Houghton Mifflin Harcourt, 2019.

Fritz, Charlotte, Allison M. Ellis, Caitlin C. Demsky, Bing C. Lin, and Stephanie Guillory. "Embracing Work Breaks: Recovering from Work Stress." *Organizational Dynamics* 42, no. 4 (2013): 274–280. https://doi.org/10.1016/j.orgdyn.2013.07.005

Gallup. *Employee Burnout: Causes and Cures.* Washington, D.C.: Gallup, March 2020. https://www.gallup.com/workplace/287060/employee-burnout-causes-cures.aspx

Gallup. *Wellbeing: The Five Essential Elements.* By Tom Rath and Jim Harter. New York: Gallup Press, 2010.

Gollwitzer, Peter M. "Implementation Intentions: Strong Effects of Simple Plans." *American Psychologist* 54, no. 7 (1999): 493–503. https://doi.org/10.1037/0003-066X.54.7.493

Gollwitzer, Peter M., and Paschal Sheeran. "Implementation Intentions and Goal Achievement: A Meta-Analysis of Effects and Processes." *Advances in Experimental Social Psychology* 38 (2006): 69–119. https://doi.org/10.1016/S0065-2601(06)38002-1

Graybiel, Ann M. "Habits, Rituals, and the Evaluative Brain." *Annual Review of Neuroscience* 31 (2008): 359–387. https://doi.org/10.1146/annurev.neuro.29.051605.112851

Hafenbrack, Andrew C., and Cassie Mogilner. "Both Work and Rest Are Moral: The Implications of Morality in Managing Productivity." *Journal of Personality and Social Psychology* 121, no. 5 (2021): 942–964. https://doi.org/10.1037/pspa0000282

Harvard Health Publishing. "Blue Light Has a Dark Side." Harvard Medical School, May 2012. https://www.health.harvard.edu/staying-healthy/blue-light-has-a-dark-side

Harvard Health Publishing. "Mindful Eating: Savoring Each Bite." Harvard Medical School, February 15, 2021. https://www.health.harvard.edu/staying-healthy/mindful-eating-savoring-each-bite

Helliwell, John F., Richard Layard, and Jeffrey Sachs, eds. *World Happiness Report 2013.* New York: UN Sustainable Development Solutions Network, 2013. https://worldhappiness.report/archive

Higgins, E. Tory. "Self-discrepancy: A theory relating self and affect." *Psychological Review* 94, no. 3 (1987): 319–340. https://doi.org/10.1037/0033-295X.94.3.319

Holt-Lunstad, Julianne, Timothy B. Smith, Mark Baker, Tyler Harris, and David Stephenson. "Loneliness and Social Isolation as Risk Factors for Mortality: A Meta-Analytic Review." *Perspectives on Psychological Science* 10, no. 2 (2015): 227–237. https://doi.org/10.1177/1745691614568352

House, James S., Karl R. Landis, and Debra Umberson. "Social Relationships and Health." *Science* 241, no. 4865 (1988): 540–545.
https://doi.org/10.1126/science.3399889

Howell, Ryan T., and Graham Hill. "The Mediating Role of Psychological Needs in Assessing the Relationship Between Spending Money on Others and Happiness." *Personality and Social Psychology Bulletin* 35, no. 12 (2009): 1609–1620.
https://doi.org/10.1177/0146167209347483

Kahneman, Daniel, and Angus Deaton. "High Income Improves Evaluation of Life but Not Emotional Well-Being." *Proceedings of the National Academy of Sciences* 107, no. 38 (2010): 16489–16493.
https://doi.org/10.1073/pnas.1011492107

Kaplan, Stephen. "The Restorative Benefits of Nature: Toward an Integrative Framework." *Journal of Environmental Psychology* 15, no. 3 (1995): 169–182.
https://doi.org/10.1016/0272-4944(95)90001-2

Karpicke, Jeffrey D., and Henry L. Roediger III. "The Critical Importance of Retrieval for Learning." *Science* 319, no. 5865 (2008): 966–968.
https://doi.org/10.1126/science.1152408

Kashdan, Todd B., Patrick E. McKnight, Frank D. Fincham, and John E. Rose. "When Curiosity Breeds Intimacy: Relationship-Specific Intrinsic Motivation and Self-Expansion." *Journal of Personality and Social Psychology* 91, no. 5 (2006): 977–991.
https://doi.org/10.1037/0022-3514.91.5.977

Kernis, Michael H., and Brian M. Goldman. "A Multicomponent Conceptualization of Authenticity: Theory and Research." *Advances in Experimental Social*

Psychology 38 (2006): 283–357.
https://doi.org/10.1016/S0065-2601(06)38006-9

Killgore, William D. S. "Effects of Sleep Deprivation on Cognition." *Progress in Brain Research* 185 (2010): 105–129. https://doi.org/10.1016/B978-0-444-53702-7.00007-5

Killingsworth, Matthew A. "Experienced Well-Being Rises with Income, Even Above $75,000 per Year." *Proceedings of the National Academy of Sciences* 118, no. 4 (2021): e2016976118. https://doi.org/10.1073/pnas.2016976118

Kintsugi: The Japanese Art of Embracing the Imperfect. Japan House London, 2019. https://www.japanhouselondon.uk/discover/stories/kintsugi-the-art-of-embracing-damage

Kivimäki, Mika, and Ichiro Kawachi. "Work Stress as a Risk Factor for Cardiovascular Disease." *Current Cardiology Reports* 17, no. 9 (2015): 630. https://doi.org/10.1007/s11886-015-0630-8

Koren, Leonard. *Wabi-Sabi: For Artists, Designers, Poets & Philosophers*. Stone Bridge Press, 2008. (Contains references to kintsugi as part of the wabi-sabi philosophy.)

Kristeller, Jean L., and Ruth Q. Wolever. "Mindfulness-Based Eating Awareness Training for Treating Binge Eating Disorder: The Conceptual Foundation." *Eating Disorders* 19, no. 1 (2011): 49–61. https://doi.org/10.1080/10640266.2011.533605

Lally, Phillippa, Cornelia H. M. van Jaarsveld, Henry W. W. Potts, and Jane Wardle. "How Are Habits Formed: Modelling Habit Formation in the Real

World." *European Journal of Social Psychology* 40, no. 6 (2010): 998–1009. https://doi.org/10.1002/ejsp.674

Lupien, Sonia J., Bruce S. McEwen, Megan R. Gunnar, and Christine Heim. "Effects of Stress Throughout the Lifespan on the Brain, Behaviour and Cognition." *Nature Reviews Neuroscience* 10, no. 6 (2009): 434–445. https://doi.org/10.1038/nrn2639

Mark, Gloria, Daniela Gudith, and Ulrich Klocke. "The Cost of Interrupted Work: More Speed and Stress." *Proceedings of the SIGCHI Conference on Human Factors in Computing Systems* (2008): 107–110. https://doi.org/10.1145/1357054.1357072

Maslach, Christina, and Michael P. Leiter. *The Truth About Burnout: How Organizations Cause Personal Stress and What to Do About It.* San Francisco: Jossey-Bass, 1997.

Mason, Ashley E., Jennifer Daubenmier, Wolf Mehling, Elissa S. Kristeller, Ruth Wolever, Frederick Hecht, and Margaret Chesney. "Reduced Reward-Driven Eating Accounts for the Impact of a Mindfulness-Based Diet and Exercise Intervention on Weight Loss: Data from the SHINE Randomized Controlled Trial." *Appetite* 100 (2016): 86–93. https://doi.org/10.1016/j.appet.2016.02.009

Mayo Clinic Staff. "Chronic Stress Puts Your Health at Risk." Mayo Clinic, July 12, 2022. https://www.mayoclinic.org/healthy-lifestyle/stress-management/in-depth/stress/art-20046037

Mazmanian, Melissa, Wanda J. Orlikowski, and JoAnne Yates. "The Autonomy Paradox: The Implications of Mobile Email Devices for Knowledge Professionals." *Organization Science* 24, no. 5 (2013): 1337–1357.

McEwen, Bruce S. "Physiology and Neurobiology of Stress and Adaptation: Central Role of the Brain." *Physiological Reviews* 87, no. 3 (2007): 873–904. https://doi.org/10.1152/physrev.00041.2006

McEwen, Bruce S. "Protective and Damaging Effects of Stress Mediators." *New England Journal of Medicine* 338, no. 3 (1998): 171–179. https://doi.org/10.1056/NEJM199801153380307

McKinsey & Company. *Help Your Employees Find Purpose—or Watch Them Leave.* New York: McKinsey & Company, April 5, 2021. https://www.mckinsey.com/capabilities/people-and-organizational-performance/our-insights/help-your-employees-find-purpose-or-watch-them-leave

McMains, Sarah A., and Sabine Kastner. "Interactions of Top–Down and Bottom–Up Mechanisms in Human Visual Cortex." *Journal of Neuroscience* 31, no. 2 (2011): 587–597. https://doi.org/10.1523/JNEUROSCI.3766-10.2011

Mednick, Sara, Ken Nakayama, and Robert Stickgold. "Sleep-dependent Learning: A Nap Is as Good as a Night." *Nature Neuroscience* 6, no. 7 (2003): 697–698. https://doi.org/10.1038/nn1078

Meshi, Dar, Diana I. Tamir, and Hauke R. Heekeren. "The Emerging Neuroscience of Social Media." *Trends in Cognitive Sciences* 19, no. 12 (2015): 771–782. https://doi.org/10.1016/j.tics.2015.09.004

Monsell, Stephen. "Task Switching." *Trends in Cognitive Sciences* 7, no. 3 (2003): 134–140. https://doi.org/10.1016/S1364-6613(03)00028-7

Montag, Christian, and Andreas Heinz. "The Addictive Potential of Social Media." *International Journal of Environmental Research and Public Health* 15, no. 12 (2018): 1–6. https://doi.org/10.3390/ijerph15122988

Mueller, Pam A., and Daniel M. Oppenheimer. "The Pen Is Mightier Than the Keyboard: Advantages of Longhand Over Laptop Note Taking." *Psychological Science* 25, no. 6 (2014): 1159–1168. https://doi.org/10.1177/0956797614524581

NASA. "NASA Nap Study." National Aeronautics and Space Administration, 1995.

National Sleep Foundation. "Napping." National Sleep Foundation, 2022. https://www.thensf.org/napping

Neff, Kristin D., and Christopher K. Germer. "A Pilot Study and Randomized Controlled Trial of the Mindful Self-Compassion Program." *Journal of Clinical Psychology* 69, no. 1 (2013): 28–44. https://doi.org/10.1002/jclp.21923

Norton, Michael I., Elizabeth W. Dunn, and Lara B. Aknin. "From Wealth to Well-Being? Money Matters, but Less Than People Think." *Journal of Positive Psychology* 3, no. 4 (2008): 264–273. https://doi.org/10.1080/17439760802399331

Palmer, Catherine A., and Ronald E. Dahl. "Sleep and Emotion Regulation: An Organizing, Integrative Review." *Sleep Medicine Reviews* 31 (2017): 6–16. https://doi.org/10.1016/j.smrv.2015.12.006

Pew Research Center. *Teens, Social Media and Technology 2022*. Washington, D.C.: Pew Research Center, August 10, 2022. https://www.pewresearch.org/internet/2022/08/10/teens-social-media-and-technology-2022

Pew Research Center. *Millennials overtake Baby Boomers as America's largest generation.* Washington, D.C.: Pew Research Center, April 28, 2020. https://www.pewresearch.org/fact-tank/2020/04/28/millennials-overtake-baby-boomers-as-americas-largest-generation

Prager, Karen J. *The Psychology of Intimacy.* New York: Guilford Press, 1995.

Przybylski, Andrew K., Kou Murayama, Cody R. DeHaan, and Valerie Gladwell. "Motivational, Emotional, and Behavioral Correlates of Fear of Missing Out." *Computers in Human Behavior* 29, no. 4 (2013): 1841–1848.

Reis, Harry T., and Philip Shaver. "Intimacy as an Interpersonal Process." In *Handbook of Personal Relationships*, edited by Steve Duck, 367–389. New York: Wiley, 1988.

Reis, Harry T., and Arthur Aron. "Love: What Is It, Why Does It Matter, and How Does It Operate?" *Perspectives on Psychological Science* 3, no. 1 (2008): 80–86. https://doi.org/10.1111/j.1745-6916.2008.00065.x

Rhodes, Ryan E., Gert-Jan de Bruijn, and Christopher J. Matheson. "Habit in the Physical Activity Domain: Integration with Intention and Action Control." *Journal of Sport & Exercise Psychology* 32, no. 1 (2010): 84–98. https://doi.org/10.1123/jsep.32.1.84

Rogers, Robert D., and Stephen Monsell. "Costs of a Predictable Switch Between Simple Cognitive Tasks." *Journal of Experimental Psychology: General* 124, no. 2 (1995): 207–231. https://doi.org/10.1037/0096-3445.124.2.207

Sapolsky, Robert M. *Why Zebras Don't Get Ulcers.* 3rd ed. New York: Holt Paperbacks, 2004.

Saxbe, Darby E., and Rena Repetti. "No Place Like Home: Home Tours Correlate with Daily Patterns of Mood and Cortisol." *Personality and Social Psychology Bulletin* 36, no. 1 (2010): 71–81. https://doi.org/10.1177/0146167209352864

Schultz, Wolfram. "Multiple Dopamine Functions at Different Time Courses." *Annual Review of Neuroscience* 30 (2007): 259–288. https://doi.org/10.1146/annurev.neuro.28.061604.135722

Schwartz, Shalom H., and Anat Bardi. "Influences of Adaptation to Communist Rule on Value Priorities in Eastern Europe." *Political Psychology* 18, no. 2 (1997): 385–410. https://doi.org/10.1111/0162-895X.00062

Seligman, Martin E. P., and Mihaly Csikszentmihalyi. "Positive Psychology: An Introduction." *American Psychologist* 55, no. 1 (2000): 5–14. https://doi.org/10.1037/0003-066X.55.1.5

Seligman, Martin E. P., Tracy A. Steen, Nansook Park, and Christopher Peterson. "Positive Psychology Progress: Empirical Validation of Interventions." *American Psychologist* 60, no. 5 (2005): 410–421. https://doi.org/10.1037/0003-066X.60.5.410

Sonnentag, Sabine, and Charlotte Fritz. "Recovery from Job Stress: The Stressor-Detachment Model as an Integrative Framework." *Journal of Organizational Behavior* 36, no. S1 (2015): S72–S103. https://doi.org/10.1002/job.1924

Sweller, John. "Cognitive Load During Problem Solving: Effects on Learning." *Cognitive Science* 12, no. 2 (1988): 257–285. https://doi.org/10.1207/s15516709cog1202_4

Teixeira, Pedro J., Eliana V. Carraça, David Markland, Marlene N. Silva, and Richard M. Ryan. "Exercise, Physical Activity, and Self-Determination Theory: A Systematic Review." *International Journal of Behavioral Nutrition and Physical Activity* 9, no. 1 (2012): 78. https://doi.org/10.1186/1479-5868-9-78

Trougakos, John P., and Alex B. Bakker. "Building Resource Capacity at Work: How Taking Breaks Can Help." *Academy of Management Perspectives* 34, no. 4 (2020): 455–467. https://doi.org/10.5465/amp.2017.0104

Twenge, Jean M., and W. Keith Campbell. "Associations between screen time and lower psychological well-being among children and adolescents: Evidence from a population-based study." *Preventive Medicine Reports* 12 (2018): 271–283.

Twenge, Jean M. *Generations: The Real Differences Between Gen Z, Millennials, Gen X, Boomers, and Silents—and What They Mean for America's Future.* Atria Books, 2023.

Twenge, Jean M., et al. "Increases in depressive symptoms, suicide-related outcomes, and suicide rates among U.S. adolescents after 2010 and links to increased new media screen time." *Clinical Psychological Science* 6, no. 1 (2018): 3–17.

Uchino, Bert N. "Social Support and Health: A Review of Physiological Processes Potentially Underlying Links to Disease Outcomes." *Journal of Behavioral Medicine* 29, no. 4 (2006): 377–387. https://doi.org/10.1007/s10865-006-9056-5

Ulrich, Roger S. "View Through a Window May Influence Recovery from Surgery." *Science* 224, no. 4647 (1984): 420–421. https://doi.org/10.1126/science.6143402

Van Breda, Adrian D. "Resilience Theory: A Literature Review." Pretoria: South African Military Health Service, 2001.

Vohs, Kathleen D., Roy F. Baumeister, Brandon J. Schmeichel, Jean M. Twenge, Nicole M. Nelson, and Dianne M. Tice. "Making Choices Impairs Subsequent Self-Control: A Limited-Resource Account of Decision Making, Self-Regulation, and Active Initiative." *Journal of Personality and Social Psychology* 94, no. 5 (2008): 883–898. https://doi.org/10.1037/0022-3514.94.5.883

Vohs, Kathleen D., Yajin Wang, Francesca Gino, and Michael I. Norton. "Rituals Enhance Consumption." *Psychological Science* 24, no. 9 (2013): 1714–1721. https://doi.org/10.1177/0956797613478949

Wood, Alex M., P. Alex Linley, John Maltby, Michael Baliousis, and Stephen Joseph. "The Authentic Personality: A Theoretical and Empirical Conceptualization and the Development of the Authenticity Scale." *Journal of Counseling Psychology* 55, no. 3 (2008): 385–399. https://doi.org/10.1037/0022-0167.55.3.385

World Health Organization. *Burn-out an "occupational phenomenon": International Classification of Diseases.* Geneva: WHO, May 2019. https://www.who.int/news/item/28-05-2019-burn-out-an-occupational-phenomenon-international-classification-of-diseases

World Health Organization. *COVID-19 pandemic triggers 25% increase in prevalence of anxiety and depression worldwide.* WHO News Release, March 2, 2022.

https://www.who.int/news/item/02-03-2022-covid-19-pandemic-triggers-25-increase-in-prevalence-of-anxiety-and-depression-worldwide

World Health Organization. *Mental Health in the Workplace: Information Sheet.* Geneva: WHO, 2019. https://www.who.int/mental_health/in_the_workplace/en/

World Health Organization. *Occupational Health: Stress at the Workplace.* Geneva: WHO, 2020. https://www.who.int/news-room/questions-and-answers/item/ccupational-health-stress-at-the-workplace

Xie, Lulu, et al. "Sleep drives metabolite clearance from the adult brain." *Science* 342, no. 6156 (2013): 373–377.

✤ About the Author

Fickle Flashes Collective is a one-woman creative studio dedicated to living gently in a world that glorifies hustle. Through reflective writing, cozy design, and honest storytelling, Fickle Flashes Collective creates books, journals, and merchandise reminders that encourage slowing down, softening up, and showing up as you are.

Rooted in the belief that rest is resistance and softness is strength, the Collective explores themes of gentle rebellion, neurodivergent awareness, midlife renewal, and the everyday magic of dogs, coffee, and calm.

Soft Rebel, Untamed Life is the first book in this growing body of work—a love letter to anyone ready to live with more meaning and less noise.

You can find Soft Edit Collective by Fickle Flashes on Etsy, where each creation reflects the same cozy, rebellious spirit that inspired this book.

www.ingramcontent.com/pod-product-compliance
Lightning Source LLC
LaVergne TN
LVHW041219080426
835508LV00011B/1001